HOW TO RAISE

RAISE

Perfectly

IMPERFECT

KIDS

AND BE OK WITH IT!

Published by Familius LLC, www.familius.com

Familius books are available at special discounts for bulk purchases, whether for sales promotions or for family or corporate use. For more information, contact Familius Sales at 559-876-2170 or email orders@familius.com.

Library of Congress Cataloging in Publication Data

2019903707

ISBN 9781641701617
Ebook ISBN 9781641702485

Printed in the United States of America

Edited by Michele Robbins, Peg Sandkam, and Alison Strobel
Cover design by Derek George
Book design by Maggie Wickes

10 9 8 7 6 5 4 3 2 1

First Edition

HOW TO RAISE

RAISE

Perfectly

IMPERFECT

KIDS

AND BE OK WITH IT!

Real Tips & Strategies for
Parents of Today's Gen Z Kids

Lisa Sugarman

with DEBRA FOX GANSENBERG, MSW, LICSW

. . . because life's not a straight line and neither is parenthood.

To my Sugarpeople—Dave, Riley, and Libby—the most perfectly imperfect family I know. Thank you for putting up with my crazy for all these years. I couldn't love you more if I tried.

—Lisa Sugarman

To the Ganz Gang; Wally, Jake, Ben, and Adam: you are the reason I smile in the morning, have happiness all day, and feel satisfied each night.

—Debra Fox Gansenberg, MSW, LICSW

Contents

Preface

Over the last twenty-plus years, I've spent a huge chunk of my time around kids. Between being the mom of two daughters and working in an elementary school for over twelve years, I've spent more than two decades learning what makes kids (and parents) tick. And what I see, more often than anything else, are kids cracking under the pressure of their parents' unrealistic expectations—expectations that they outdo the kids around them in every conceivable way. I also see parents worrying *way* too much about how their kids' success or failures will reflect on them. And that's created a toxic subculture of stressed-out kids and stressed-out parents.

As a result, kids are seeing specialists in record numbers and being medicated to control everything from anxiety disorders and depression to social phobias and panic attacks. According to the *2016 Child Mind Institute Children's Mental Health Report*, 17.1 million young people under the age of eighteen have or have had a diagnosable psychiatric disorder, and that number continues to rise.[1] These are scary stats if you're a parent.

I've spent almost half my life watching kids (and parents) fall apart around me when they didn't make the team or win MVP or get into their first choice Ivy League school. And lemme tell you, it's gut wrenching, because these kids can't cope with anything less than perfection . . . and neither can their parents.

You've noticed, I'm sure, that helicopter and bulldozer and lawn-mower parents are everywhere, with kids being micromanaged by hyper-competitive moms and dads, leaving no real time for them to just be kids. And I'll bet, without even thinking twice, you can rattle off a list of parents you know who are overscheduling their kids so that every available second of their day is crammed with activities. You may even be doing some of it yourself without realizing it.

As the author of the nationally syndicated opinion column *It Is What It Is* and the *Boston Globe* Local Bestseller *LIFE: It Is What It Is*, I've spent the better part of the last ten years reminding people that **life is always a work in progress** and that no one's perfect and we're not supposed to be. Especially kids. What today's parents need more than anything is a wake-up call to dial down their intensity and let their kids just be kids while they can. And if that means making some mistakes along the way, then so be it.

In my opinion, too many of today's parents have trouble accepting that it's okay—and even necessary—to let their kids screw up. It's like they've forgotten that one of the most important skills we can impart to our children is the ability to make mistakes, learn from them, and keep moving forward. But too many parents are afraid of the consequences of letting their kids fall, worried that they won't be able to get up on their own.

I wrote *How To Raise Perfectly Imperfect Kids . . . And Be OK with It* to give parents tactical, proven strategies and advice for embracing the imperfections of parenthood. Because, until now, there's never been a parenting book—or better yet, a survival guide—dedicated to helping moms and dads pull back just enough to let their kids make mistakes and learn from them.

Along with Dave, my husband of over twenty-five years, I've weathered every stage of parenthood, from finding that little red plus sign on the pregnancy test to sending my oldest off to college. And I'm still standing. (We're still standing.) And so are our kids. What I've learned through it all is that life—*especially parenting*—is never the straight line we imagine it to be as we're starting out. Instead, parenting is an uneven road, littered with muddy sinkholes and full of detours we never expect. But it's also one helluva beautiful ride. We just need to accept that we're not going to be perfect parents and our kids aren't going to be perfect kids—and that's okay, because we're not supposed to be. Instead of worrying about perfection, we can give our kids the tools to accept failure and keep going; and that can do more to help unlock their true potential than you'd ever imagine.

With *How To Raise Perfectly Imperfect Kids . . . And Be OK with It*, you'll learn the survival skills to navigate the rough waters of parenthood and avoid the common challenges of raising kids in a hyper-competitive world. As your personal guide, I'll share some of my proudest momming moments, some of my heartbreaks, and some of my challenges and triumphs to help you understand why one of the best things we can do for our kids—and ourselves—is to take a step back and give them the reins. Because, sometimes, the most valuable gift we can give our kids is the ability to let them help themselves.

And the sooner we embrace that, the better off we'll all be.

Introduction

How do you raise *the perfect child?*

Uh, *you don't.* Sorry.

Yet parents everywhere are still trying to raise their kids to be smarter, faster, more successful, and more popular than their peers. They're bringing them up to believe that failure just isn't an option, oblivious that what they're really doing is setting up their kids to crash and burn.

As the mom of two grown daughters, I know it's not easy to go from zero to six hundred overnight when we become parents. But that's exactly what parenthood is—the ultimate baptism by fire. One day it's just you and your deliciously warm down comforter sleeping in on a cold Sunday morning, and then it's not. Before you know it, you've got tiny people hopping onto your bed at five o'clock in the morning, prying open your eyelids, and begging for pancakes. And then you're "on" until one of you loses steam twelve to eighteen hours later.

At the same time that parenthood upends our lives in every possible way, it also starts us on the most beautiful and challenging journey that most of us will ever take. Like most journeys, it's much easier to find our way when we have some sort of a road map to guide us in the right direction, offering *just* enough direction to ensure that we don't drift too far off course.

In case you haven't noticed, most maps are one-dimensional representations of the real world. They don't give us the *local knowledge* we really need to get around and survive. You know, those hidden details that show us where all the bumps are and how to avoid them, stuff that only a local would know. Well, I'm your local, and this is your new survival guide that'll help you stay nimble when you hit unexpected detours that threaten to knock you off course.

I created this "map" to help you stay on course and to give you a glimpse of what lies ahead, so you can avoid the pitfalls of trying to be the perfect parent and raise the perfect kid.

In it, I talk about everything from social and emotional growth to cognitive development, as well as major developmental milestones in between and how to handle them. I break things down into short, funny, survival tips that explore the real issues we all deal with when we sign on to be parents. And I help you find the humor and beauty in raising perfectly imperfect kids.

With the help of my lifelong friend, Debra Gansenberg, MSW, LICSW, founder and president of New Beginnings Counseling Service, P.C., we offer a toolbox filled with strategies, tips, and language to remind parents that life with kids is chaotic, even on the best of days, but learning to be flexible with whatever life throws at us is our biggest asset as parents.

Whether you're a new, expectant, or experienced parent, the goal shouldn't be to raise perfect kids, but instead to raise well-adjusted adults who can handle whatever life throws at them with grace, courage, and a great sense of humor.

Onward friends . . .

How to Use This Book

Understand one very important thing . . . I don't have all the answers for how to survive parenthood. What I *do* have is a book full of proven **strategies** and **approaches** that I've used, and watched other parents use, that will help you dial down your stress level while you juggle the challenges of parenthood.

And I've got one more thing—something wonderful. I call her the book's special sauce. Someone who counterbalances my mom-in-the-trenches perspective with the clinical side of parenting to give you a true survival guide for navigating parenthood. Debra Fox Gansenberg, MSW, LICSW, founder and president of New Beginnings Counseling Service, P.C., out of Boston, pipes in in each chapter to give parents tangible tools. The wife and mom of three boys, she's a veteran family systems therapist with twenty-five plus years of experience counseling children, adults, families, couples, and parents.

When you see the couch icon at the end of every chapter or sprinkled within, get comfy and take a seat, because you're in the therapist's office with Debra and she's giving you her clinical perspective on everything I talk about, chapter by chapter.

We invite you to turn to this book as an everyday reminder that you're not the only one out there with a hormonal, impulsive, immature, lunatic for a kid. Reach for it whenever your son or daughter pushes you to the brink. Grab it when you need someone to relate to when you're questioning yourself as a parent. Read it when you just need to bond with someone who's gone through it all before and come out the other side. Or just hang onto it so it keeps you from falling over the edge and into the abyss.

Read it to remember that you're not alone . . . to remind you that all children test their limits . . . that this too shall pass . . . and that your kids will ultimately turn out just fine. We swear.

And if for nothing else, use it to wedge your bedroom door shut so your kid(s) can't get in the room.

The Power of Positivity Is Every Parent's Secret Weapon

We can't always control what our kids throw at us, but we can *definitely* control how we react to it, and leading with positivity can make *all* the difference.

Being a parent is hard. And I'll never try to sugarcoat it, because it's just the reality of bringing up kids. What I *will* tell you, over and over and over again throughout this book, is that your attitude is *everything* when it comes to raising kids. That's why the overarching theme throughout every chapter of *How to Raise Perfectly Imperfect Kids* focuses on harnessing the power of positivity and using it to our advantage on our journey as moms and dads. And it's our ability to choose happiness that's our most useful tool as we head out on the long and beautiful haul of parenthood.

Imagine it like this: Our attitude is like a giant suit of bubble wrap that insulates and protects us from all the rough spots we hit with our kids. While it can't stop things from happening around us, it *can* help cushion us from some of the emotional shots to the head that we take as parents. Our attitude is one of the only things we have complete control over, and it's one of our biggest assets. See, positivity is a conscious choice, and when we practice happiness as parents and coach our kids to do the same, then, eventually, they'll learn to choose it on their own.

Since our kids don't just pop out of the womb wired for positivity, the whole concept of attitude needs to be taught and then modeled and then reinforced with an epic amount of practice. *Tons and tons of practice.* Just like we influence how our kids learn manners or good study habits or how to pee on the potty, we're also the ones responsible for shaping their understanding of what it means to have a good attitude. And we do that by modeling it ourselves. We lead by example.

It's up to us to explain to our kids that happiness is a choice—probably one of the most important choices any of us can make. I mean, as far I'm concerned, happiness is a life skill—a skill we learn first at home. In fact, teaching it to our kids and then helping them hone it is 100 percent our responsibility as parents. And we need to nail it. Fortunately, there are plenty of ways to do it, and teaching by example is at the top of the list. We're the role models for our kids, so what we say and how we say it and what we do and how we do it influence the way our kids interact with one another and the rest of the world. So, if we're super conscious of the language we use when we're talking to other people, that type of language will imprint on our kids. If they hear us encourage and support and praise the people in our lives, then it's a solid bet that they're going to do the same, you know.

> 🛋 **It is important to understand how your family system operates due to the fact we all impact each other. Teach each other about yourself, you might be surprised at what you learn!**

Another powerful way we teach our kids is by letting them know when we screw up and owning it when it happens. Because it's by reinforcing the reality that nobody's perfect that our kids can accept that mistakes are inevitable—for all of us. Then they won't be traumatized when something goes wrong. Instead, they'll be able to rally, learn from their mistakes, and get back in the game. Look, if we could make one wish for our kids, I'll bet the majority of us would wish for them to be happy. I know I would. In fact, it's the one thing I've always wished for my girls. Because, at the end of the day, our ultimate goal in raising our kids is to raise healthy, *happy* little people who grow up to be content and positive grown-ups—adults who can then take what they learned from us, put their own unique and beautiful spin on it, and pay it forward in their own families someday. And so on, and so on.

Because I want to help families be the best version of themselves that they can be, I designed a book that captures the essence of what it's like to raise kids in their natural environment and allows us to be happy while we do it. I want to offer parents a resource—like a field guide—that speaks to the perfectly imperfectness of raising kids and gives parents the tools and strategies and confidence to navigate through the weeds and raise happy, healthy humans.

Above all else, I want to remind parents that it's okay to screw up as we raise our kids. In fact, it's *exactly* what we're supposed to do.

Molding who our kids are and how they perceive and interact with the world is a big job, and it happens mostly under our roof. So we need to make sure that they understand, from as early on as possible, that everything they say or do can almost always go one of two ways: positively or negatively. Either they've got a cup that's half full or one that's half empty—the way they see it is up to them. And the way they learn to see it is up to us.

We're all a product of where we come from—especially our kids. If we aspire to raise well-adjusted and happy kids, then we have to create that kind of environment for them at home—and we have to support it by being positive—ourselves. We can't just walk around saying one thing and doing another. We can't complain about work or grocery shopping or the ironing or mowing the lawn every week and then expect our kids to willingly and happily sit down and do their math homework. We need to model all those things ourselves.

Walk the Walk

Our ultimate goal is to raise happy, loved, and motivated kids, right? Well, the way we do that is by engaging with them and showing them the way. We need to teach them, by example, what it means to choose happiness in their everyday lives and why it's such a powerful skill to learn. Because when our kids see us encourage and support and inspire the people around us, then our kids will be motivated to do the same.

I'm a big believer that happiness is a trickle-down effect, especially in families. It starts from the top—from the parents—and trickles its way through everyone else. This is exactly why it's so critical that we model happiness early on with our kids. Because kids tend to follow our lead with most things, especially the positive stuff. Like how our daughters won't ever get off the phone without saying "I love you." It's something they picked up from us, because Dave and I have always done that with each other and with them, and now it's become part of their DNA.

In the case of my own childhood, my mother had an awful lot she could've been down about considering she was suddenly widowed at forty with a ten-year-old daughter at home. She could've been mad at her situation, depressed, salty even, and no one would've blamed her under the circumstances. That anger or disappointment or feeling of being overwhelmed could have easily filtered down to me. But she made a different choice. She stayed positive in the face of extreme loss and pushed on. While she never hid her sadness, she made sure it was heavily tempered by her ability to still focus on all the positive pieces of her life—of our life. She did little things like sing or hum all the time. Still does. I was constantly being hugged and kissed and cuddled and loved. She made an effort to see the positive side in everything. And she made sure I knew that even though there's extreme sadness and disappointment in life, it's balanced by immense joy and beauty and happiness if we just let it in.

I see the results of my mom's example of happiness in my ability to be positive, and I see it in the attitudes of kids I've worked with over the years. I've watched kids come into school every day who always project happiness and contentment because they have parents who encourage it at home. Every day. In school, on the soccer field, at home. Everywhere. These are the kids whose attitude is so consistently positive and upbeat simply because they have someone guiding them at home, modeling the same kind of outlook. *Practicing* it with them day after day. We'll talk more about how this works as you practice it day after day and see happiness become a real part of you and your kids. Because while life isn't always rainbows and unicorns every minute of every day, the more often we make the deliberate choice to be positive, the more likely that will become our mood's default setting.

Personally, I find negativity toxic and a complete turn-off, as far as qualities go. Now sure, we're all entitled to be moody or sad, but when those moments become a regular pattern, then we've got a problem.

4

Like the mom of one of my daughter Riley's friends who used to trash-talk her daughter to me every chance she got. Her daughter felt the punch of negativity every time a hurtful word came out of her mom's mouth. As a result, the older the girl got, the more prone she was to hurling the same negativity at her own friends. It was no surprise when she became a product of her environment.

On the opposite side, there are the moms I know who always make an effort to use positive language to point out a problem or bad behavior with their kids. These are the parents who understand that children aren't born knowing how to handle themselves in every situation. They need to be taught. These are the parents who give their kids the chance to correct mistakes or bad decisions by gently pointing out what they do wrong and how they can change their behavior for the next time. If their kids say or do something that isn't okay, instead of making a scene and being harsh, these are the parents who talk to their kids from a place of sensitivity and love, and that makes all the difference in the world because their kids don't feel criticized or belittled. These parents calmly and carefully talk to them in a way that shows respect and compassion. They focus on using positive and constructive language and give them the tools to make better decisions next time.

It's just not possible to teach our kids how to be joyful unless we're happy ourselves. We're the single most powerful role models for happiness that our kids will ever have. So, if we don't project authentic happiness and contentment, then our kids will never learn to do it themselves. If we're constantly whiney and intolerant and judgmental, then we should naturally assume that that behavior will rub off on our kids. On the flip side, if we project joy, patience, and acceptance, we should assume that behavior will rub off. So, we need to watch ourselves and how we behave around them. We need to keep our moods in check and stay conscious of the attitude that we project. Because our kids are watching and absorbing and copying and regurgitating. Every. Single. Second.

📖 **Parents need to check in with the meaning behind their own actions before they make their next move.**

Practice Makes Close to Perfect

It's like I've said: happiness is a skill. And all skills—like our numbers and letters and how to drive—need to be taught. There's no denying that the process of fusing those skills into our hardwiring takes time and patience. It just does. In the same way that we have to hang onto the back of our kid's bike seat while they're learning to ride without training wheels, we have to nurture our kid's happiness. And to do that, we teach them to use tools like positive self-talk, developing gratitude, and finding joy in doing everyday things. Eventually, when they learn how to stay happy on their own, we get to just step back and watch them live what they've been taught.

Before that happens, we need to teach our kids to make positive thinking a habit. And we do that by encouraging them to believe they can do anything as long as they have the right attitude. We motivate them to see the good in every situation, so that when they're challenged by something negative, their internal positivity helps them push through.

This is just like when my mom made the conscious decision to go back to college to get her degree only six months after losing my dad. I remember her sitting me down and telling me that she had been dreaming of going back to school since she was eighteen. She had gone to work right out of high school to help support her family and regretted never getting her college degree. She said it was going to take time and feel incredibly uncomfortable, and it would be a massive balancing act, but that it would make our life better in the end. She said it was waaaay outside her comfort zone but she had to go for it. So she did. She stayed positive and committed and made it happen. And in the process, she taught me that there was nothing I couldn't do if I just dug in, stuck with it, and kept grinding.

It's the same when our kids are learning something new like a tricky math concept or how to pull off a backbend; we remind them that it's not going to click right away because learning takes time and practice. We help them gag their inner voice that says they can't and help them replace those feelings of negativity with a big fat dose of positivity. We encourage them to stick with it—whatever "it" is—and to reach out for help and ask questions and put in their best effort. We need to teach them to expect that they're going to struggle or fail or fall, but the only way to make progress is to keep getting back up and staying in the game.

Learning takes time and practice. Encourage your kids to stick with it, whatever "it" is.

📖 **It's not easy to know when to draw the line when it comes to a commitment.**

When our kids are confronted with challenging people in their lives—mean kids or adults who push their buttons or get under their skin—we need to arm them with the knowledge that they can't control what the people around them say or do, because that's out of their hands. Instead, we teach them that we're in control of how we react to what happens around us. They can choose to get angry and lash out and say or do something that they'll regret, or they can decide to take a step back and regroup or walk away or reach out to someone for help. Because that's the ultimate key here. Then we just keep reminding them (until they're sick of hearing the sound of our voice) that how they handle themselves is always *their* choice.

📖 **Learning how to tolerate and manage differences is important in today's world.**

It's a given that our kids aren't perfect. Just like Mom and Dad, they make mistakes. But we can teach our kids that even our mistakes are opportunities to hone their positivity skills. We need to help our kids understand that mistakes are moments to learn and they can choose to do better the next time. After all, corny as it sounds, practice really does make perfect.

Mistakes are moments to learn.

Choose Happiness

My kids have grown up hearing me say over and over (and then over again) how attitude is literally *everything*. Ev-er-y-thing. Our attitude is one of the few things in life that we have complete control over. It's that one thing that isn't dependent on anyone else—the one thing we almost always have the ability to **choose** to access. When our kids are young all we can do is keep reinforcing the simple idea that they can choose to make themselves miserable or allow themselves to be happy in any situation. (Not easy, even as simple as it sounds here in black and white.) So, we need to encourage that idea every chance we get. Because it takes a long, long time before our kids develop a consistently positive outlook that allows them to squash their tendency to be pouty snots.

Like when we go to work every day, we can either choose to embrace the job we have to do and consciously give our best effort or choose to be negative and depressing and a buzzkill. But that choice is ours and ours alone. And *our* choice will speak volumes to our kids.

Our kids can be upset that they're leaving the park or choose to be happy that they got to stay as long as they did. They can be mad that it's time to go to bed or choose to be happy that we're going to snuggle with them and read them a bedtime story. And it's our job to keep showing them the positive angle, because kids don't often see that on their own, especially when they're young. But they do get there. Ultimately, they figure out that **choosing positivity is like a superpower**—almost like having a shield that can repel just about anything negative. And one of our most important parenting jobs is to teach our kids how to harness that power.

Choosing positivity is like a superpower—for parents and kids.

Eventually, with time, our kids develop the bandwidth to understand that they can almost always choose happiness. In any situation. At school, with friends, on the soccer field. Everywhere. And that when they make that conscious choice to stay focused on the positive side of a situation, they'll always be in control. And then happiness becomes like one of those ugly orange life preservers tied around their neck that keeps them from sinking into negative places.

I know with my own girls, I had to constantly remind them that having a positive attitude makes life easier all around. Whenever one of my kids came home from school in a bad mood or had a fight with a friend or tanked a test, I'd remind them that they had the ability to cut those negative feelings loose before they could fester and grow and affect the dynamic of the rest of the family. I was forever giving them mini happiness lessons to help them turn their mood around by encouraging them to remember that they could always choose to be happy or reach out to their friend and talk it out or use a different study strategy the next time around. I'd remind them that the more they practice being positive, the easier it would be to stay positive when frustrating stuff happened.

I used to explain to my girls that it was always okay to be sad or mad or frustrated about something, as long as they worked through it and got to the other side. Because holding on to negativity does only one thing—it triggers more negativity. It's like a toxic game of dominoes. Inevitably, when one of my kids was in a nasty mood, it always managed to permeate the rest of the house. One person would snap at someone and then it was a chain reaction of snippiness. And before we knew it there was a seismic mood shift in the house and everyone was nasty. Even Mom.

Fortunately, though, choosing happiness works the exact same way, because it's uplifting, positive, and feels good to be around. For the same reason that one person's laughter can infect a whole room with laughter or a flash mob can spark everyone to dance, happiness can re-wire our homes and even our brains.

So, there it is: **Happy parents breed happy kids**. (In most cases.) And unhappy parents breed unhappy kids. (In most cases.)

Now sure, genetics represent an awful lot as far as predetermining who we are physically and emotionally, but I also feel strongly that we're products of where we come from. I mean, it's simple math that if a child comes from a troubled home, the likelihood of that same kid being troubled themselves is high. On the flip side, it's just as logical to assume that a child who comes from a happy, loving, supportive home stands a better-than-average chance of becoming a well-adjusted, happy adult. And I believe it because I've seen firsthand the equation play out both ways.

See, we're the ones our kids are watching and copying and idolizing, so it's on us to lead by example. It's our job to set the mood in the house by doing things like encouraging optimism and practicing gratitude and using positive language. Because that's what it takes to help them learn to walk the walk themselves. It takes consistency and dedication and some long-term modeling. Remember, as parents, we're in it to win it. And it's a labor of love. So, we need to constantly focus on those positive behaviors as much as we need to reinforce that they shouldn't cut off someone's ponytail or drop f-bombs at the dining room table.

Remember . . .

Happy kids are motivated kids.

Happy kids are more productive kids.

Happy kids are more expressive kids.

Happy kids are more communicative kids.

Happy kids are more fulfilled kids.

Happy kids are more empowered kids.

We have to remember that life is mixed with a wide range of emotions and the only way to ensure that our kids are prepared for what's out there is to let them experience as much as possible. That means they have to experience the highs, as well as the lows. Because the only way to really ensure that our kids know how to handle certain things is to actually let them experience the widest range of emotions we can. We can't insulate them from the life around them. Our kids need to feel the pain and the bliss and the success and the disappointment in life in order to learn how to maneuver through it when the time comes.

The irony is, that as desperately as we all want to raise our kids to be happy and joyful, we have to also raise them to accept the reality that life isn't always that big, overflowing bowl of cherries. That there's disappointment woven into every phase of life. But that's okay, because disappointment teaches us all good lessons too.

The simple, unfiltered truth is that life—including parenthood—isn't a straight line. But when we're armed with a positive attitude, we can almost always find our way to the other side of just about any situation. And when we give our kids a foundation of happiness, love, and support, they'll have the tools they need to grow into healthy, happy, well-adjusted people—and eventually, grown-ups and parents themselves. Positivity is the gift that keeps on giving and will help them as they lay the foundation for a happy life.

You are going to sleep well at night knowing you've passed on the super power of a positive attitude.

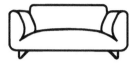

From the Couch of
Debra Fox Gansenberg MSW, LICSW

It is important to understand how your family system operates due to the fact we all impact each other. Teach each other about yourself you might be surprised at what you learn!

Pleasure and satisfaction are wonderful parts of life as they are feelings that lead to happiness. We have to remember to communicate our mood and emotion through verbal and non-verbal communication. Again, we must lead by example. If we are always hunting for ants instead of looking up to the stars, it can become contagious. If you want to see your child full of joy and happiness you must exemplify those same things. "Chin-up," "Smile," and "Turn that frown upside down," are all great ways to encourage a child to reach toward happiness. Be mindful of what you are communicating through body language and facial expression.

Tip: Be mindful that happiness looks and sounds different for everyone. Make sure you aren't assuming that your child isn't happy or, by mistake, think they are. We need to be careful that children, like adults, can be feeling one thing inside but paint on a different face for those watching in order to please or dismiss what could be going on inside that doesn't feel so good.

- Teach feeling words and match them with pictures of facial expressions or their reflection in the mirror in order to communicate more successfully.
- Ask questions: "How are you feeling?" "Tell me what that smile is about." "If your tears could talk, what would they say?"
- Create some fun and playful activities in the home that can enhance the mood and create joy and happiness: A dance party every Friday afternoon or a tea party to chit-chat for younger children, or a game of floor hockey or pool for older children, will create a sense of playfulness that can end a busy day with a smile.

Tip: Call a family meeting to discuss how each person understands their own moods and behavior. Teaching each other about yourself is priceless. Then have each family member explain how they experience the others in the family and describe how their mood or actions can impact them. Consider enlisting a family therapist to help with the process, it can be invaluable.

Tip: Asking each other "What do you need?" is a tool which can help to manage and understand family members' emotions and needs. Sometimes we think we know what another person needs and go ahead and do it, but what we think they might need and what they actually need could be different. Save your time and energy and ask what is needed first. You might be surprised.

Parents need to check in with the meaning behind their own actions before making the next move.

Tip: A key to parenting success is for us to keep our *parent parts* in check—the part of us that doesn't want to see them struggle needs to step back so our child can locate the part of them that can stay motivated and dedicated to those things that might challenge them. Then, locate the parent part that can support and guide your child through the difficult stuff. Learning how to deal with challenges as a younger child is necessary. Guide your child as they develop skills that will help them cope and manage themselves as they grow older.

Tip: Remind yourself that failure is okay. Update your old belief system that says failure is bad. It might not feel great, but it is what you do with the failure that really counts. Get curious with your child about how to forge ahead and make the struggle or failure count. What is a valuable take away?

- One way of looking at failure as valuable is the actual experience. Experience under your belt helps you with anything the next time around. How will you approach these failures differently when confronted with them again?
- Failure can help mold a child's ability to feel compassion and appreciation when there is a successful achievement. When things come too easy or too often, children may not realize how special the accomplishment is.
- Teach your kids not to worry about what others are thinking.

Reframe their failure as stepping stones. Encourage modeling a graceful trip over failure by showing others how a not-so-great outcome can look okay. Remember that you have to believe what you preach. Your children will survive and so will you!

It's not easy to know when to draw the line when it comes to a commitment.

Tip: When it comes to sticking with a commitment, we need to consider our child's age and the nature of the commitment. It is easier to help a child get through a difficult commitment if they have choices. For example, "You signed up for guitar lessons and see you don't like them. How about you complete the ones I have already paid for and then try something else?" When it comes to school-age children there is more flexibility to the commitment; however, as children enter the teen years, you really need to help your teen understand that seeing their decision through is important and discuss the consequences for not sticking with it. For example, if they are part of a team and they begin with a losing season and they drop out, teammates are not going to see them as a reliable and supportive teammate. Sometimes healthy peer pressure can teach some of the hardest lessons kids need to learn. Parents can step aside at times and use the child's own peer group as the third-party to do the job of teaching.

Learning how to tolerate and manage differences is important in today's world.

Tip: When there is a difference of opinion, a difference in approach, or a difference in feelings about something or someone, we need to teach our children tolerance. Model a Stop, Think, and Do approach to tolerance. Encourage kids to stop and observe and listen and think about what they have experienced, and then share how it makes them feel or what they think. Your goal here is to encourage space dedicated to openness and reflection so that difference is tolerated successfully.

Message: All parts are welcome: angry, sad, frustrated, et cetera, and we are here to help, not hinder, your process.

Survival Tip 2:

Don't Get Caught in the Comparing Trap

Our kids don't all learn how to ride a bike on the same day, but they do figure it out eventually.

As parents, we do a lot of comparing of our kids, both to their own siblings (if they have them) and to the kids around them. Especially once they hit school age. We intentionally and unintentionally measure them against their brothers or sisters and other kids because we just can't help ourselves. We're curious about how other kids are growing and maturing and adapting, and we want to ensure that our own kids are staying on track with the kids around them. And yeah, on some level, we're also a little competitive. *Can't be havin' Jen's kid swimming without a swim bubble before my kid!*

Because today's parents are so hyper-focused on making sure that their kids excel at everything, it's tricky to know when to pull back and let them grow at their own pace and when to push. And that's got a lot of us in knots because no one wants to watch their kid get lapped by everyone around them. As a result, parents everywhere are micromanaging their kids and putting too much pressure on them to outperform their peers, whether our kids are up for it or not. With so many different developmental milestones to check off, both in and out of school, a lot of parents are ignoring where their kids are developmentally and focusing instead on where they think they ought to be to measure up.

I mean, how many times have you said to yourself, *Why isn't my kid reading yet? How can the Smith kid* possibly *be reading chapter books already?! Why can't* my *daughter ride a two-wheeler yet? How come my son can't throw to first base? Why isn't my kid as tall as the other kids in his class?* I get it, because *I've been that mom*, thinking those exact same thoughts. It's impossible not to. And anyone who says they haven't is flat-out lying. But what we absolutely should *never* become is the mom or dad who calls our kid out to her face for not being as fast or as smart or as strong as all the other kids. That's like a cardinal sin of parenting.

📖 **Avoid comparing siblings at all costs, it will cause your kids to develop an inferior/superior dynamic, and that's dangerous territory.**

Once we put our kid in the mix with a whole bunch of other kids, that natural inclination to compare kicks in. So do yourself a favor and don't be too freaked out if you're doing it, because we all do it to some degree.

It's one thing to talk privately to our husband or wife about concerns we have about our son or daughter's social or emotional or academic issues, that's cool. Being aware and in tune with our kid's development is just good parenting. It's what we're supposed to do. But talking smack about our kids, in front of them, is totally not okay. Then you're sending a very clear-cut message to your child that it's not okay for them to develop at a speed that's comfortable for them. Then you're kicking them directly in the bull's-eye of their self-esteem, which says that they're not measuring up.

We all want the best for our kids. Obviously. We want them to succeed and thrive and excel, but they're not going to do that according to someone else's pace. They're only going to do it when they're ready. Trying to force it only creates animosity between you and them. To set unfair expectations according to how other kids develop is just unrealistic and sets an awful precedent. Which is exactly why we need to embrace our kids exactly where they are. We need to let them feel our support and our patience, because when they know they have that, that's when they start blossoming. And when they think they don't have our support and acceptance, that's when they wilt. It's when they start paying too much attention to what everyone around them is doing that the big-time inferiority complex usually surfaces.

We need to let them feel our support and our patience, because when they know they have that, that's when they start blossoming.

Don't Be *That* Parent

Being in the school system for so long, I saw a disturbing number of parents shooting down their kids for not making the varsity team or high honor roll or getting the MVP award. And it was tough to watch. I've had kids as young as first-graders admit to me that they thought their dad liked their older brother better than them because the older brother could hit the ball farther. I also know plenty of siblings who were openly compared against each other—friends of my own kids. These were parents who made no secret of the fact that they expected their younger child to play the same sport, at the same level, as their sister. Whether they were into the sport or not. So, along with creating performance anxiety in their kid, they also forged a rivalry between siblings that could damage their relationship in the long run.

Like the dad I bumped into at the park one day when my girls were still young. He had played college football and felt the need to unload on me how inadequate he felt that his son sucked at Pop Warner ball. He said his daughter could play better. He just couldn't let it go. And all I could think of was *poor kid to live in that shadow.* Or the gymnastics mom I used to sit next to at tumbling who would complain about her daughter not being able to do a cartwheel. Made her daughter feel horrible in front of all the other girls, not to mention the other moms. She criticized her every time the girl tumbled by. It was awful, but imagine what it must've felt like to be her daughter? No big surprise that the little girl quit gymnastics altogether after that class.

It's healthy for us to measure our kids against other kids their age as a way of helping us keep track of the age-appropriate stages our kids are cycling through. But it becomes a very *bad* thing when it morphs from casual observation into nitpicking and criticism.

I've watched dads scream at their sons for not tackling the receiver hard enough and heard moms belittle their daughters for letting in a goal *that the other goalie could've stopped*. And every time I see it, it makes me ill because it makes the kids feel like inadequate losers.

With Dave as a soccer coach for over twenty seasons and me coaching cross-country since 2012, we've both seen our share of kids getting reamed by their parents for not scoring enough points or running fast enough or trying hard enough. And trust me, it doesn't get any easier to see each time we're confronted with it. We need to do ourselves and our kids a favor and not get too hung up on where everybody's at on the learning curve. Because, in most cases, they all get to where they're supposed to be eventually. Just at a slightly different pace. But they most definitely won't get there through intimidation and bullying.

It's just common sense that we shouldn't be comparing our kids to anyone, and certainly not to their face. It's counterproductive and it's hurtful. And it leaves an indelible mark. That's because doing too much comparing only gives our kids an inferiority complex and that's a pretty heavy weight to bear as a kid. Because when a little girl feels inadequate, it's almost inevitable that she'll become a young adult who feels insecure and then, ultimately, a self-doubting grown-up. And we all know that hollow feeling of thinking we don't measure up. It can wreck us.

It's sad, really, that so many parents are more hung up on their kids performing well, or better than their peers, than they are concerned with their kids being *truly happy*. And that's because, unfortunately, a lot of parents are competitive and see their kids as a reflection of themselves. If they were captain of the basketball team, they expect their kid to play hoops and to be good at it too. So when their kids don't perform well, they take it as a personal slam—almost like they've failed somehow as a parent.

Grown-ups need to realize that our kids pick up on our approval as much as our disapproval. Disapproval even more, I think. Which is why we need to celebrate their strengths and help support their weaknesses. We need to empower them to take their time and work hard at what they love. And we need to be okay when our thing isn't their thing.

We need to celebrate our kid's strengths and help support their weaknesses.

📖 **Be careful, as comparing can translate to approval or disapproval.**

Let Your Kids Find Their Groove

The real truth is, we all need to relax. Our kids are okay, whether they can hit the ball as far as their friends can or not. They're okay if they don't learn how to tread water on the same day that all the other kids do. They're okay if they aren't drawing masterpieces in the third grade.

You've heard of late bloomers, right? Well, my oldest was one and she's doing just fine. Better than fine, actually. Not to brag, but . . . she made the Dean's List her freshman year of college and is successfully involved with more extracurricular activities than our whole family combined. And I'm telling you this for a very specific reason. Because at our first parent–teacher conference when Riley was in preschool, her teacher told us to consider holding her back. Apparently, she did everything on what they called "Riley Time" and didn't always want to stop doing whatever she was doing when it was time for everyone to transition. Pretty normal for a four-year-old, but the concern was that she would fall behind.

Dave and I went back and forth about what to do, worried that if we didn't hold her back we'd be setting her up to fail further down the line. But, ultimately, we took a step back and decided not to have her repeat preschool. We felt, at the time, that everyone blossoms at different times, and she barely had one foot in the door at school yet, so we shouldn't judge where she was at too prematurely. And man, were we glad we let her move on. Because eventually she found her mojo.

Worth mentioning, too, is that Riley couldn't draw more than a stick figure until she was in the eighth grade. But since she had no interest in going to art school, we didn't put too much emphasis on her being able to draw a still life as well as the other kids. Instead, we let her focus on playing the violin and learning how to ski, and eventually she caught up. When the desire was there, she caught up. And that's key. When our kids start discovering the things that inspire them, they usually turn on the jets and really start moving. She also played soccer from the time she was in kindergarten, all the way up to high school. Loved the sport. Loved that Dave coached her. Loved that she got to run around every day on a big field with her friends. But never scored a goal in a regular-season game in her entire career as a player. But that didn't hold her back. That didn't impact her. Instead, when she got to high school, she decided to try something new. Decided to try running cross country just to be part of a team. And wouldn't you know, the kid who ran a ten-minute mile her freshman year became captain of the cross country team her senior year and walked off as a six-minute miler.

Oh yeah, and when she was halfway through the eighth grade, one of Riley's artsy friends taught her the basics of drawing portraits and that changed everything for her. Something clicked and this artist emerged that none of us knew was inside her. So much so that she was inducted as a member of the National Art Honor Society her senior year of high school. I mean, who knew? More proof that sometimes it's just about timing. Especially with kids.

That's the thing. It's sometimes hard to distinguish between a kid who's falling behind and a kid who just hasn't found her groove yet. Because in a lot of cases, our kids just haven't found their rhythm, so it's a challenge for us to know when there's a legitimate problem and when they're just not interested in something. That's why we have to be diligent, faithful observers, constantly watching and supporting as they literally unfold before us.

I know, we want to ensure that our kids are keeping up with their peers and not getting too behind the eight ball. That's normal. And wanting that doesn't make us bad parents. We just have to remember that kids—all kids—develop different skills at different paces and at different times. And that's okay. Focus on my words . . . *that's okay.*

Find What Lights Your Kid's Fire, Then Fan Those Flames

In our role as our kids' moms and dads, one of our primary jobs is to encourage them to pursue what inspires them and teach them not to care about keeping up with the people around them. We're supposed to push them to follow their own unique path and send a consistent message that *they* get to decide what they like and, just as important, that their best is enough. 'Cause believe me, as a soccer mom I watched plenty of miserable little kids running up and down the field complaining about how much they hated soccer. All they wanted to do was swim or play basketball or ice skate. But for whatever reason their parents pushed soccer.

> 🛋 **Encourage your kids to pursue what inspires them and not worry about what other people are doing.**

Now don't misunderstand, I'm not suggesting that our six- and seven-year-olds get to drive the bus and call all the shots in terms of what they do. They are still just kids who need a gentle kick in the a** some of the time. But what I am saying is that at some point, after we've done our job exposing them to different things and encouraging them to mix it up, we should respect them if they don't make a love connection with a particular sport or activity. We need to teach them to honor the commitment they make to their team or group, but after that's over, if they're still not feeling the love, they can try something else. And we should always support that.

The bottom line is that our kids aren't born knowing what they like. They need to get their noses in there and try everything they can. So they should play all the sports and sample all the groups and do all the things before they have a real sense of what truly clicks for them. And that's okay. Kids are just naturally going to compare themselves to the people around them, because that's just a piece of the figuring-it-all-out process. What we should really be doing is relaxing a little and giving our kids the chance to experiment and try things on to see how they fit. Because while we might think something looks good on them, like a lacrosse uniform or a field hockey stick, they're the only ones who can really decide what *feels right*.

Just Relax

Too many parents worry about looking bad if our kids aren't performing at the same level as the kids around them. I remember one of my girlfriends almost throwing up in her mouth when she heard my daughter Riley (five at the time) reading beginner reading books. She was in a frenzy over the fact that her daughter, who was a little older than Riley, wasn't stringing words together yet. And she just couldn't let it go. She wanted to get her daughter tested for a learning disability, stat, just because her daughter wasn't at the exact same reading level as my kid. Caaa-ray-zeee! And she didn't hold back saying any of that in front of her daughter, who was frustrated enough because she couldn't read.

Needless to say, some of the other moms and I had to have a little intervention to stop her from hurtling off the deep end and running straight to the Special Ed Chair at the School Department. We reminded her that if her daughter is a little ahead or even a little behind with some skills, it's perfectly normal. And that with the right kind of support and nurturing at home and in the classroom, most kids will catch up to the crowd. (Just as a point of fact, that same girl graduated high school with my daughter a couple of years ago and went on to an Ivy League school. Just sayin'.)

Unfortunately, the underlying problem with a lot of parents is that they take it personally if their child is a little behind. Like they're actually embarrassed that their son can't drain a free throw or draw a house that looks like a house. Or that their daughter can't Hula-Hoop like the other girls. And when our kids are constantly being compared to other kids, that insecurity eventually has an impact—and not the good kind.

The fact is, an awful lot of growth happens between the ages of five and eight. A lot. And then again during middle school. And yet again during the high school years. But again, not all kids will start doing the same things at the same time or at the same speed. All. Kids. Are. Different. Remember that and don't torture yourself if your kid can't pump as high as all the other kids can on the swings.

It's only when *we* let go of the idea that our kids need to do certain things at certain times that our kids can be free to develop in their best way. They need to know that we're okay with them hitting their stride at their own pace. When our kids are free to develop without unfair expectations, that's when they can really thrive.

We're the first teachers our kids have, so if we put unreasonable expectations on them to do things before they're ready, we're setting them up for failure down the line. If we compare them to everyone around them, we're ensuring they develop an inferiority complex. And if we judge them too harshly for not being able to keep up, we're going to crush their self-esteem. So, it's up to us to adapt to their pace even though we often think we know what's best for them. And since we don't get an owner's manual when our kids are born, learning what their pace is is more or less trial by fire.

Remember, some kids jump straight to walking and never crawl. Some kids read in kindergarten, some don't. Some kids potty train in one shot, others just keep pooping in their pants for weeks. But they *do* get there. And since the pace that they get there is already imprinted on their DNA from the get-go, we need to quit comparing them and start embracing them. So relax. Love your kid for who and where they are right here and now. Forget about what the kids around them are doing and focus your energy on helping your child learn at a pace that works for them.

Give them the space and freedom to grow and they'll love you for it. I promise. Then they'll do exactly what goldfish do when you put them in a giant fishbowl with a ton of space to grow: they'll flourish. And that's *exactly* what you want.

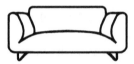

From the Couch of
Debra Fox Gansenberg MSW, LICSW

Avoid comparing siblings *at all costs*, it will cause your kids to develop an inferior/superior dynamic, and that's dangerous territory.

Tip: Understand what part of you needs to compare your child to others. Have that part gain awareness that this behavior is impacting their self-esteem, self-image, self-confidence, and overall mental health.

Tip: Some comparison is fine when we use it to measure developmental milestones . . . but if parents are constantly doing it then it becomes damaging for everyone.

Tip: When you compare siblings, you're teaching your kids that life is about competition and comparison, which is not healthy and leads to a decreased output from your kids on many levels.

Tip: Understand the impact of comparing—it reduces kids' motivation and desire to try, increases anxiety, and decreases self-worth.

Message: We all want what's best for our kids, which means that it starts with us and our behavior. Be mindful of the amount of comparing you do and the reasons you're doing it. Kids hear and see loud and clear when they are being compared, and nothing good comes of it!

Be careful, as comparing can translate to approval or disapproval.

How often do you remember a time when you acted out of the desire for approval from your loved one? Some might even agree that as adults they *still* might base their decisions on "What will Mom and Dad think?" As parents, we want our kids to make decisions that are what *they* need, not what *we* need them to be. Recall a time that you felt disapproval, judged, or rejected by a loved one. What feelings or thoughts do you recall? Where do you feel those things in your body? Is your stomach upset? Is your heart racing? Is there a heaviness throughout your body? Do you feel headachy? None of these things feel good. What can you do to impact your child's emotional well-being in a positive way when it comes to approval?

Tip: Find the part of you that remembers what it was like to seek approval. Now when you interact with your child, see if you can act from that part in order to find the words, body language, and facial expressions that will help your child feel heard, accepted, and validated. The impact of our verbal and non-verbal behavior is *so* important.

Tip: Avoid criticism, disappointment, or even punishment when it comes to disapproval. A child is growing and learning. Mistakes, poor judgment, and decision-making happen. Begin by being an active listener. Listen to your child and to what you hear them saying. Remember that your kids are always seeking your approval and praise and want to make you proud. So instead of speaking and sharing what you think first, be an active listener and try and understand why they're doing what they are doing in order to better understand their point of view. Listening and validating doesn't mean you agree with what they're saying. You are creating space for them to be heard.

Tip: When kids learn of their parents' disapproval and are feeling criticized, they can begin a dangerous habit of internalizing your feedback, which can lead to anxiety. They do this instead of sharing because they're assuming what your response and reaction will be based on history. Change it up and surprise them by giving them the space they need to share. Then, after listening to them, it becomes your turn to talk. Begin by reflecting back to them what you heard them say in order to gain clarity and fine-tune any confusion or misunderstanding. When they're done sharing, it's your turn to speak and share your thoughts, opinions, and feelings. Then ask your child to reflect back to you what they think they heard you say.

Tip: If you learn that your words have been harmful or upsetting to your child, loop back around and own it and apologize. Saying you're sorry can go a lot further than you realize. Apologizing can mend and repair harmful conversations or unkind words, as well as amend the times when things weren't said or done that were needed. Sometimes we don't understand just how impactful our words can really be—good, bad, or indifferent.

Message: Kids have big ears and wide eyes. They're always watching and listening, so be aware of where and who you're speaking to about your children. All they want and need is your love and approval. Remember how it felt for you to want and need these things. It's our job to give freely.

Encourage your kids to pursue what inspires them and not worry about what other people are doing.

Tip: Our expectations can lead our children in directions that they aren't interested in. Avoid judgment as it could quickly eliminate a child's interest and passion, and ultimately lead them down a path that's wrong for them.

Tip: It's our job to be the voice of encouragement and to help them think outside the box. Gain awareness and learn what your children's unique interests are and introduce them to different things. Then let them lead in their own way. Involve the whole family in the pursuit of curiosity.

Tip: Remind your kids they don't have to be a pro to do something they like. Adopt the idea that being brave enough to pursue something you love is exciting and could lead to the success. Teach your children to love exploring the possibilities. Encourage reading, playing, and singing. These are all wonderful ways to expose your children to learning and developing a variety of interests.

Tip: Eliminate the stress around "having to know" what you like and be good at it. Keep it simple. Don't overschedule and expose your kids to too much at once. Enjoy the journey of the pursuit and take your time. If you go through activities and exposures too fast, chances are you could be missing out.

Message: During the pursuit of what interests your child, keep an open mind. Be supportive and patient. It takes time for kids to find their passion. It might not be something you're interested in, but give your child the space to find their own way.

Your Kid's EQ Is More Important Than Their IQ

Being book smart is great, but it's the kid with high emotional intelligence who's really gonna crush it at life.

From the day they're born, we start building a laundry list of things we want for our kids. We want them to be healthy, to have a great temperament and rock-solid social skills. We want them to be smart and well-adjusted and kind, and instinctively know how to keep their rooms clean, among soooooo many other things. Although when you dissect the list carefully, there's one thing we often forget, and that's EQ: Emotional Quotient, or emotional intelligence. We forget that we also want them to be able to recognize, gauge, manage, and express their emotions. Oh, and the emotions of all the people around them, too. And it's ironic that we forget to consider EQ so often because it's actually what many experts today consider the special sauce of the human personality.

Psychcentral.com says EQ "is the ability to identify, use, understand, and manage emotions in an effective and positive way. A high EQ helps us communicate better, reduce our anxiety and stress, defuse conflicts, improve our relationships, empathize with others, and effectively overcome challenges. Our emotional intelligence affects the quality of our lives because it influences our behavior and relationships."[2]

And by contrast, our Intelligence Quotient (IQ) is a standardized way of measuring a person's ability to reason academically. In other words, it's a test that compares us to our peers and gauges our intelligence against the people around us. So EQ and IQ are two totally different animals. EQ focuses on our emotional connection to the world around us, while IQ is the score we get on a big, fancy aptitude test.

So what I don't get is that if our EQ enables us to do all those things, why isn't growing our kids' EQs considered a priority across the board? Especially since IQ does none of those things.

Now it's a given that both EQ and IQ are invaluable qualities that can, in large part, make or break our kids' future. The question is, though, is one more important than the other? And is it the one we've all been trained to expect?

I know we were all taught when we were young that education is everything. *Pay attention in school, get good grades. That's how you'll make something of yourself.* A good education will propel us to a bright future. To a huge degree, that's true. But what I've also learned as a mom is that there are a lot of more critical traits associated with raising a solid kid than we realize. Being book smart is only one, and it may not even be the most important one.

In my opinion, our EQ is one of the *most* crucial and underrated strengths we can develop. I mean, what good is it having a card-holding Mensa member for a kid if they can't look someone in the eye while they're talking? Or if they don't have the ability to empathize with people? Or if they can't be a good friend? Because all of those things matter. They matter a lot. Some may say they matter the most. Often it's not until we raise kids ourselves that we realize how much a strong EQ really matters in life.

In her CNN Health article, "Understanding Emotional Intelligence and Its Effects on Your Life," author Erin Gabriel says, "the ability to read, understand and respond to emotions in ourselves and other people is a crucial factor in predicting our health, happiness, and personal and professional success."[3]

Raising two of my own daughters and watching them grow and engage with other people along the way, I've come to realize the value of having kids who can relate to the world around them. Because children who can read social cues and express themselves well (and actually emote) are a real commodity in a world where today's kids do most of their interacting screen-to-screen, instead of face-to-face.

I've seen kids who couldn't control their emotions, not because they had behavioral issues but because they just lacked a healthy emotional infrastructure. I've dealt with kids who were incapable of making emotional connections with other kids because they just didn't understand other people's feelings. I've watched kids lose friend after friend because they just couldn't keep their emotions in check. They'd scream at someone or be overly critical or toss out an insult without thinking twice. And even though these kids might score well on tests and be smart according to academic standards, they don't understand how their actions affect the people around them.

Look, I know in a perfect world we'd all love to raise a son or a daughter with the total package—a high EQ and an equally high IQ. We'd all love our kids to be book smart and have good social skills, a strong sense of responsibility, good judgement, and a big heart. That's the ultimate goal. But no one's perfect and there's no such thing as the perfect child. Realistically, most people end up being a combo of all those things.

Now that I have the perspective of being a parent for almost twenty years, I can honestly say that I don't feel like enough emphasis has been put on the EQ side of our kids' growth and development, on raising kids who are emotionally well-balanced and secure.

Sure, a person's IQ measures their raw intelligence. But it's pretty much just based on one-dimensional test scores. On being able to interpret and process and regurgitate what we read in books or what we learn from teachers. Our EQ, though, is our sense of street smarts. It's being able to use our common sense to handle the world around us. And I don't know, maybe it's just me, but I kinda think that might trump just about everything else. Because part of the beauty of EQ is that a lot of it can be taught and practiced at home.

We've all heard stories about the Doogie Howser–like kids who weren't being academically challenged in their age-appropriate grade, so their parents skipped them ahead so they wouldn't be bored. And I'll just say this: They might be ready one way, but that doesn't mean they're ready in all the ways that count. Just because they can keep up with older kids on paper, doesn't mean they're emotionally ready to jump ahead.

I'm using this as an example for the simple reason that we have to acknowledge, when our kids are still young, that even though we live in a culture that's hyper-focused on academic excellence, it's not the only thing that's important as we raise our kids. When the motivation to see them succeed intellectually outweighs the desire to see them thrive emotionally, we're setting ourselves (and them) up for problems. It takes waaaay more than just book smarts to be successful. Kids need the total package of academic and social and emotional and physical maturity to be able to make it. We can't just hammer at them about test scores and report card grades. They need to know that there's more to life than being able to score well on tests. Being the smartest person in the room doesn't matter if no one wants to sit with you at lunch because you don't know how to relate to anyone.

> 📖 **Developing our EQ is something that is critical to our success in the big world. The beauty of EQ is that a lot of it can be taught and practiced at home.**

Raising a kid with a solid EQ means they have what's called *situational awareness*, which, in simple terms, means that they know what's going on around them and they can adapt to changes in their environment like a boss. That ability and confidence to collaborate with the people around them is invaluable, along with the ability to communicate, de-escalate conflicts, and sympathize and empathize with others. So, developing a high EQ is a top-tier life skill as far as I'm concerned.

And I feel so strongly about EQ being such an important quality that if we could only choose to have a child with one of the quotients, I'd pick EQ. No contest.

In my case, I was the kid who didn't have a natural aptitude for learning flat, one-dimensional stuff. I was the visual kid, the one who needed pictures and hands-on interactions with the material I was learning in order to make it stick. I was not a naturally brainy kid, like a lot of my friends. I struggled to learn dates and concepts and formulas and always felt like I spent twice the amount of time everybody else did trying to be successful academically.

But I worked hard. Really, really hard. And I was organized. I was the kid who stayed after school for help and did the extra credit and threw my hand up every time my teacher asked a question. And to this day, I believe it's those things that carried me through. Being diligent made all the difference for me in terms of being able to stay with the pack and not fall behind. That diligence and awareness that I needed to study in a different way than my peers is part of EQ. EQ was my advantage. And I leveraged it as much as I possibly could.

See, I figured out early on that it was going to have to be my people and organizational skills and drive that would sustain me, not my raw IQ. And so far, so good.

According to John M. Grohol, Psy.D., at *PsychCentral*, "Intelligence Quotient, or IQ, is a theoretical construct used by psychologists within standardized tests as a means of describing one's intelligence level"[4] (that is, how much information we can assimilate). On the flip side, PsychologyToday.com says a person's EQ "refers to the ability to identify and manage one's own emotions, as well as the emotions of others."[5] Basically, EQ helps us build and maintain relationships and understand ourselves and those around us. And that's a pretty big deal in the grand scheme of life.

What I'm suggesting is that, as parents, we need to work to focus on the whole child, not just on the one who's going to need to apply to college somewhere down the line. Because while being a high academic achiever will definitely open lots of doors for our kids later on in life, it won't ensure that those doors stay open. We also have to consider how that same kid is feeling when academic pressure is applied in the wrong way or at the wrong time. I've seen the other side of that parent pressure up close, and it's a pretty ugly thing to watch. Working for so many years around kids, I saw how constant pressure to perform affected kids in some pretty profound ways, like causing eating disorders and anxiety, sleep disorders, and depression. And the kids I'm talking about weren't even middle school or high school kids. They were elementary school kids.

I can't tell you how many grammar school parents I've encountered who were neurotic at the end of every quarter when it was time for report cards to be distributed. Those report cards don't even have traditional letter grades! You'd have thought their kids were in their senior year of high school with Ivy League acceptances depending on what was on that piece of paper.

Instead of being concerned that their kid got a *Needs Improvement* on *Follows Class Rules* or *Works Cooperatively* or *Shows Respect for Others*, all those parents cared about was that their kid got a four out of four in *Number Sense* or *Algebra and Functions*. And they'd threaten their kids with consequences or punishments if the next report card wasn't stellar.

> 💭 **Teaching your kids what a good quality of life is is important, and we do this by setting realistic and attainable goals and expectations.**

The problem is, putting that kind of pressure on our kids can backfire. Badly. I saw countless kids implode because they were afraid of failing a third-grade spelling test. I had kids cry to me that their mom was going to yell at them if they didn't get a good grade on a math test. I've had kids go to the nurse's office, day after day, with a stomach ache that was actually just stress manifested as real pain. All because their moms and dads thought that grades were the most important thing. And that's sad, because they're not.

For me, though, those *Social Skills* and *Listening and Speaking* sections were always where my eyes went when I ripped into that envelope every quarter. Because those are the things that matter most. Knowing that our daughters could relate to their peers and treat their teacher with respect was of paramount importance to us. And we told our girls that's what mattered the most.

From the time they understood what grades and report cards were, we told our girls that we expected their best effort in school—whether that effort resulted in straight As or straight Cs. Because, in the end, not everything comes easily to everyone. We all learn in different ways and to different degrees. But effort is effort, and a strong work ethic can compensate a lot for weaknesses in other areas, like book smarts.

Our kids need good interpersonal skills and communication skills to be successful in life too—whether grade school, middle school, high school, college, or beyond. They need to be critical thinkers and have the ability to be nimble and to ask questions and to read people and situations. They need to be able to multi-task and manage their time and take criticism and accept failure. They need to know how to do a lot.

So, what can we as parents teach our kids to really prepare them for real-life success—not just test success? We can actually teach EQ skills: things like strong self-image, the ability to play well with other kids, and knowing how and when to listen and how to stay in control when we're on the edge. If our kids think that the only thing we care about is the grade on a paper or whether or not they make the honor roll, then we're sending a damaging message that could have a pretty catastrophic impact as they get older.

> 📖 **Focus on teaching your children to build and maintain relationships. Relating to people is much more important than getting an A in science.**

As a kid who almost always tested poorly on any kind of standardized test, I've always felt strongly that academics alone just aren't a true indicator of a person's ability or potential. There are *so* many other facets to our personality that I don't think it's fair to assume that a transcript full of grades is more important to a person's overall success than their ability to relate well with people or their ability to be kind or listen to a friend, or understand themselves and what they need to do to excel.

Now don't get me wrong, of course there's a part of me that would love to be like Madonna and have an IQ of 140 and have a glossy Mensa membership card in my wallet. But when it really comes down to it, that Intelligence Quotient is not what I really think we need the most to be successful in life. It's important, no doubt, but when we really break it down, having a high IQ offers absolutely no guarantee that we'll lead a successful life. And while I totally recognize that it opens certain doors that may otherwise have stay closed, a high IQ is no guarantee that you'll be able to keep your high-profile, high-paying job.

Truth is, if you can't relate to people, or build and maintain relationships, then you won't be in your sweet new job for very long. Because people won't like you and you'll get fired. And that's because without the vital people skills you need to function in the mainstream, you'll never be able to successfully collaborate. Remember, there's no "I" in "team" for a reason.

According to a Carnegie Institute of Technology study, 85 percent of a person's financial success is due to skills in human engineering, which includes your personality and your ability to communicate, negotiate, and lead. And, shockingly, only 15 percent is due to technical knowledge.[6] Kinda makes you think and gives what I'm talking about a little more credence, doesn't it?

With our girls, we always emphasized that it's their effort that matters most. Sure, we push them to work hard and aim as high as they can, and sometimes that doesn't translate to an A or a perfect score. Sometimes our kids' academic best is just going to be mediocre, but that doesn't mean that they've failed. It just means that their strengths lie elsewhere. And it's up to us to empower them with the emotional strength to find them.

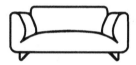

From the Couch of
Debra Fox Gansenberg MSW, LICSW

Developing our EQ is something that is critical to our success in the big world. The beauty of EQ is that a lot of it can be taught and practiced at home.

Tip: Be different; create a home culture that rewards empathy, compassion, thoughtfulness, and kindness instead of just academic excellence. Observe your child's behavior, name it, and then acknowledge it so your child understands what they are doing: "Adam, it was so thoughtful of you to make me a card," or "Sally, you were so kind when you gave your friend your lollipop because hers fell on the floor." You could tie the *catching someone being thoughtful* to a token economy. When a family member exhibits a form of kindness, compassion, et cetera, they can earn a token and put it in a jar. Gathering enough tokens could lead to the experience of a family reward; for example, going to the movies or a day at the water park in exchange for, say, twenty tokens. This can breed a happy, fun, and healthy family life while building an Emotional Quotient.

Tip: Create opportunities to teach your children self-awareness and self-regulation by helping them understand their own emotions so their feelings won't rule them. Create space within the family unit and time together to allow your children to express themselves and share what they are feeling: "You seem so down right now, what's going on?" or "You kicked that ball really hard, are you angry. Share with me what you are feeling." Then, after asking questions, it is your turn to be a great listener. You might not understand or like what is being said, but create the space to make it safe and okay for a child to share any type of feelings. Once your child has seen you listen calmly, it's time for you to share and model another form of good self-management.

Tip: Share your observations in a non-judgmental way so your kids can learn other people's perspective of their behavior. Don't shame them for feeling angry, but share how it looked so they can learn. They will then feel safe enough to trust their own emotions and self-expression as they get older. Once kids feel heard and that their emotions are acceptable, you will see that their acting out behaviors will dissipate and healthier ways of expressing and sharing emotions and feelings will emerge.

Tip: Don't hand everything to your children. When things are too easy, children are not motivated. They need to learn how to apply themselves and gain appreciation for hard work. Unfortunately, Gen Zers are used to everything being easily accessible, whether parents hand it to them or they locate it themselves. Help kids set goals and work hard to reach them. You can model for them this possibly through a token economy system.

Teaching your kids what a good quality of life is is important, and we do this by setting realistic and attainable goals and expectations.

Tip: Check in with yourself to see why you put so much emphasis on performance and high expectations? Life has demands and parents want kids to meet these responsibilities and be successful so their quality of life is the best it can be. For many of us parents, we put these expectations on our children and the expectations rest as burdens instead of useful information. We often do this without realizing it. As parents we need to become more self-aware and understand what "good quality of life" really means and how we teach our kids what a good life looks like and means. What is difficult is the diverse meaning behind what a good life looks like. Take time to discuss this and then share what you think is realistic with your children. Create space for them to have their own ideas and opinions about what a good life looks like to them.

Tip: As parents, we're always looking for the reason why our kids might be anxious, not sleeping, or depressed . . . did you ever stop to think it could be you, your words, your actions, and your expectations? The greatest gift you can give your child are realistic expectations. Letting go of our expectations creates space for them to develop their own. The world we grew up and the world Gen Zers are growing up in is very different. Their wild and crazy ideas and dreams might be more easily attainable and realistic because of the way the world operates today. "Never say never" is a good rule of thumb when your children are young. If you paint a negative picture, it might unknowingly dissuade your child from pursuing what they really want. As kids grow older and formulate career goals and aspirations, create space for listening and then move to reflective questioning to get them thinking about how realistic their expectations really are. It's their job to see if their expectations are attainable, not yours.

Tip: Check in with your child's teachers/school to learn accurate and age-appropriate benchmarks, homework, and expectations to help guide you. Checking in with your child and teachers is the best way to monitor what performance should look like and what expectations are reasonable. If a school is doing a good job of educating your child they will educate the whole child and pay attention to their social, emotional, behavioral, and academic performance to assist in helping you understand your child's capabilities and set realistic goals in each category.

Focus on teaching your children to build and maintain relationships. Relating to people is much more important than getting an A in science.

Tip: Create the space to be imperfect. Learning a skill like communicating is not easy; however, it is essential to grow relationships, learn, hold jobs, and succeed in several aspects of life. Remember, learning how to ride a two-wheeler often includes falling off and getting hurt until you figure it out. Learning how to share your thoughts, feelings, and emotions with another person takes lots and lots of practice too. So, slow things down at home and take time to share simple things with one another to practice and learn how to create a relationship through communication.

Tip: By sharing one's thoughts and feelings you are growing emotional intimacy, which is something quite necessary to maintain a relationship. Modeling for your children how to share your thoughts, feelings, and opinions is an invaluable gift. In turn, they will find their voice and gain confidence to share once they witness that it is okay to share these things with others. I find too often that when parents do not communicate and model this behavior, children follow suit and struggle to learn these skills later in life. Get started so your children can earn an A in growing and maintaining relationships, which will provide love and happiness for a lifetime.

Message: Having children is really all about forming relationships with them in order to create family. Family members have a special love license. It allows us to treat each other like no one else, sometimes a good thing and at other times not so much. This love license allows us to time to learn and practice how to love, communicate, and treat and respect others. It is within the confines of our family of origin where it all begins and continues for a lifetime.

We've Got to Teach Our Kids to Be Responsible

If we don't teach our kids to do things for themselves, then they won't have a clue how to manage their life when they're on their own.

I'm not sure who said it first or why (not that it matters), but whoever it was that came up with the line "there are no free rides" is my hero. Because it's true in every aspect of our lives, especially where kids are concerned. We all need to learn how to pull our own weight, both in our personal and our professional worlds, as much for ourselves and our own sense of independence as for the people we interact with along the way. And the earlier we learn that, the better off we are in the long run. This is exactly why one of the best things we can give to our kids is a sense of ownership and responsibility. In fact, the sooner we do this the better. Otherwise, we're raising a generation of freeloaders. And we can't be doing that, now can we?

I know, I know, we don't want to impose on our cute little munchkins to do too much too soon. I mean, they're so little and so inexperienced and so fragile, right? Uh, wrong. Wrong, wrong, wrong. Our kids are *way* more capable than we realize, *way* earlier than we think they are. We're just so used to caring for them and coddling them and wiping their chins (and butts) for those first handful of years that we often don't recognize when they're ready to start taking on some age-appropriate responsibilities. We see them as helpless little babies who need hand-holding, who have to keep their hands away from the stovetop, and who shouldn't help put the china away. And while that's true to a point, with the right guidance our kids can also be real contributors if we give them a chance. Without things like chores and regular tasks, our kids become entitled, and an entitled kid is B-A-D. Because an entitled kid becomes an entitled adult. And that's even worse.

It's Never Too Early (Well, Once They Can Walk and Talk a Little)

With my kids, we threw chores at them almost from the time they could walk and talk. We wanted them to feel like valuable little members of our family, so we involved them in as much of the day-to-day chores and routines as we could so they'd have a feeling of ownership in the home they were growing up in. You know, as a way of developing a sense of pride in themselves and where they came from.

We handed out the reasonable stuff in the beginning (when they were around four or five), like putting their dishes in the dishwasher and clothes in the hamper and trying to get themselves dressed (I stress *trying*, because watching a four-year-old try to manhandle a pair of tights on her own is dicey). Then, when they got a little older (like six or seven) we turned up the heat and doled out the more advanced, highly complex stuff like feeding and walking the dog and bed-making and running loads of laundry. Expanding their repertoire, you know?

Now relax, we weren't exploiting any child labor laws. We were just involving our girls in our day-to-day family routines, so they'd get a sense, early on, of how to manage the life skills that everyone needs to master by the time they go out on their own. We started when they were young because, let's face it, there's a lot to learn and the learning curve is wide. Kids don't come out of the womb knowing how to bake the perfect chocolate chip cookie with just the right amount of chew factor, properly clean the dryer filter, or correctly fold a fitted sheet. Those things all have to be practiced over and over again. For years. Starting them early eases them into the routine of doing these things regularly.

📖 **Gen Z is known as the *Entitlement Generation*. As parents, we must work hard to prevent our children from developing a sense of entitlement or unrealistic expectations.**

It's also to our advantage to let our kids get a feel for what we have to do every day as parents. Because I don't know about you, but for the longest time my kids thought a pile of neatly folded laundry just spontaneously appeared on the corner of their bureau every week; or that a team of sneaky little ninja elves snuck into their rooms every Sunday morning and changed their sheets, leaving them crisp and smelling lemony fresh; or that food cooks itself and finds its way to the kitchen table every day; or that groceries instinctively know how to travel from the supermarket into our fridge—all by themselves. We need to prove to them that all of this stuff happens manually, not magically. And the best way for them to understand that is by rolling their sleeves up and getting their noses in there.

The best way for kids to understand how all those household chores happen is by rolling their sleeves up and getting their noses in there.

By the time I was ten years old, my dad had taught me how to use a lawnmower, how to pump gas, how to change a flat, and how to pump up my own bike tires. The list is long. And my mom did the same, teaching me how to Con-Tact paper my dollhouse walls (indispensable life skill), how to bake a level birthday cake, how to water the flowers without drowning them. That list was just as long. And learning all those things just made me want to learn more things. Because I found knowledge to be power.

I can remember being seven or eight, eating at my mom and dad's favorite restaurant, begging them and our regular waitress to give me a job. All I wanted was my own little spiral order notebook and white half-apron. I wanted to clear tables and take orders and wash dishes. I mean, I would've cleaned out toilet bowls just to say I had a job. And it wasn't even about earning money; I just wanted a purpose. (Again, don't ask me why. I was a bit stupid back in the day.)

So what did my parents do? After hearing me beg for a job week after week, they secretly arranged with the waitress and the owner to let me "work" in the kitchen. And the night the waitress called me into the kitchen to "tell me something" was a defining moment for me. Because when I walked into the kitchen and she and the cooks handed me a little white apron and a notebook from the Five & Dime Store, I was finally being taken seriously. Which is really all most little kids want anyway.

They let me take people's orders (those people being my parents). They let me stack dishes and fold napkins and put ice in the glasses. In my head, though, it felt like they were trusting me with nuclear launch codes. That's how grown up I felt. And because of that, I wanted to do the best job humanly possible. Their faith in my ability to do the job (any job) inspired me. It gave me the confidence to believe I could do it and that got me inspired. For a kid, that's big.

Sure, kids balk, at times, but they're kids and that's what kids do. They just don't understand that all these seemingly mundane little chores we ask them to do all serve a purpose. These little chores like taking out the trash and making beds and doing dishes are building up to something. Doing something as simple as taking the dog out or putting away the laundry every day gives our kids the foundation for doing bigger, more impactful things for themselves and others down the line. And since it's our job to parent our kids, keeping them on task—even when they don't want to be—is just one of the many ways we do it.

📖 **Eliminate the power struggle by asking questions about why your child might be pushing back.**

Few things are more important than learning how to fend for ourselves. If we don't learn how to do that, then how can we possibly ever learn how to take care of anyone else? That's the main reason chores are so valuable. There is actually a big purpose in having our kids do these seemingly tedious little tasks. By having them do tasks over and over and over, for years, we teach our kids to be self-sufficient by the time they go out in the world on their own.

📖 **Parents, finding your patience, adjusting your expectations, and letting go are the keys to raising self-sufficient children.**

40

Working Together as a Family Creates a Team Mentality

It's only when our kids have learned a solid work ethic at home, and they understand the benefits of pitching in and pulling their weight, that we know we've done our job well. Helping out around the house is a simple and easy way for our kids to develop a sense of being a team player. And there's no team more important than the Home Team.

Until then, we need to hammer at them with this stuff so they understand that learning to keep their room clean is a life skill. Putting their dishes in the dishwasher is a life skill. Knowing how to make their whites *super* white is a life skill. Learning how to be an active contributor in life starts at home, but getting them to understand that and cooperate can be a struggle. What kid would ever opt to do chores over playing Xbox or shooting hoops or watching Netflix? No kid, that's who. Which is exactly why we need to expose our kids early on to the world of chores. We want to weave it into their lives from the time they are little to avoid any real shock to their system when they become adults.

By age five, our girls were doing hospital corners on their beds (not really, but that would've been impressive, right?), taking in groceries from the car, setting and clearing the dinner table, and helping cook meals. We wanted them to get comfortable doing all the little day-to-day things because you never fully understand what it takes to do something unless you've done it yourself. You also have no way of empathizing with someone unless you've walked in their shoes. Like, oh, I don't know, a mom or a dad. And a great way to do that is to let our kids do a little bit of heavy lifting to give them a healthy dose of perspective.

This is also around the time when it's smart to consider using an allowance as an incentive for doing regular work around the house. At five and seven, my kids were too young for any kind of real job like babysitting or a paper route, but they were definitely capable of consistently managing some chores around the house. So as a way of exposing them to what it means to work for your money, we started giving them around five dollars a week for walking the dog and doing things like dishes and taking out trash. Just a little bit of pocket money that made them feel grown up and responsible. And it worked, because they learned early on what it felt like to earn their own money. Money that didn't always come right away either, because we'd give them their allowance at the end of the week only after they did all their chores.

Granted, there have been plenty of times when they blacked out and completely forgotten that a bathrobe or towel goes on the hook on the back of the bathroom door that's specifically designated to hold them and for some reason put it on the floor (which I don't recall ever having a hook). They are kids, after all. They needed to be guided. But what I've found, now that my kids are older and self-sufficient and both holding down jobs, is that they love the feeling of being self-reliant. They like being productive and knowing how to take care of themselves. And yours will too, eventually.

The key is to start small with our kids. I say again, **we need to start**. We have to teach them that being a contributor at home isn't just great because it lightens Mom and Dad's load around the house, but that they're going to feel really good about helping out. And that the value of their contribution isn't measured by the size and scope of the chore they do, but, instead, by how much it helps everyone around them.

The value of their contribution isn't measured by the size or scope of the chore they do, but, instead, by how much it helps everyone around them.

The problem often is, though, that devoting the time it takes to show them what to do in the first place isn't always easy. Because, as we all know way too well, young kids need to be supervised almost every waking second. Even though they don't think they do, they need a certain amount of hand-holding when they're learning new things.

Now in theory, delegating responsibilities around the house makes our load lighter. In theory. But it doesn't always start out that way. Initially, when we're teaching our kids how to help us cook or do laundry or wash dishes, we need to be prepared to build in some training time. But that's the case with learning anything new. And that's definitely the case with young kids.

Investing Time in Teaching Kids to Work Will Pay Off

Just keep in mind that the extra investment of time teaching our kids how to negotiate the kitchen or the laundry room is *way* worth it on the back end, trust me. Think of it like potty training. I know, in some ways, it was almost easier to let our kids pee and poop in a diaper that kept everything self-contained than to lock ourselves in the house for a week and train our son how to use the potty like a big boy. I have countless friends who prolonged getting their daughter into big girl undies just because they didn't want to have to deal with the training process. So I get it—it's sometimes easier to just keep it simple. But we're not doing anyone any favors, least of all our kids. Because the sooner we empower them to think and do for themselves, the more capable and confident they'll be in the end.

Truth is, some parents view giving their kids chores as an inconvenience, because they have to teach and supervise them until the kids can manage tasks on their own. But those same parents aren't thinking long-term. They don't realize that, eventually, a little bit of effort on the front end almost always translates to a more self-sufficient kid on the back end.

The simple fact is that chores are good for our kids, even though our kids will insist that they aren't. Because being given adult responsibilities is empowering when we're young. It's a gesture of good faith on our part to show them that we trust them to handle real-life stuff and acknowledge that they're mature, or at least maturing. That's how I always felt, anyway. I loved the idea of working from as early as I can remember. I always wanted a job. Always wanted to be trusted to do grown-up things. (Don't ask me why. I was clearly just a confused kid who didn't recognize how good I had it as a child with little to no real responsibility. Youth . . . it's wasted on the young.)

The simple fact is that chores are good for our kids.

If we're going to be successful teaching our kids how to start fending for themselves and giving back at home, then we have to resist the urge most of us have to do everything for them. It's actually critical.

Because the longer we hand-hold, the tougher it is for our kids to let go and stand on their own. And that's the true endgame with parenting. I know, when our kids are so young and still so dependent on us for so much it's hard to ever imagine that the time will come when they'll be able to live life on their own. But it comes. And it comes fast.

So here's what *not* to do . . . Don't tell your daughter you don't need her help chopping veggies just because you're afraid she might cut herself. All of her future salad preparation depends on it. Plus, she needs to know how to cut stuff if she's going to be able to use her own kitchen someday. And don't forget: chores are gender neutral. Our daughters are just as capable of shoveling snow and raking leaves as our sons are. Our sons are just as able to switch and fold the laundry and load the dishwasher as our daughters.

The other important trap not to fall into is being too much of a perfectionist to hand off chores to our kids. It doesn't matter how our delicates get folded. They're only going under our skinny jeans or in our underwear drawer. Don't be a control freak who doesn't trust anyone. It creates incredibly negative energy and just makes you look like a martyr—no one likes a martyr. Trust me; I had to resist all those urges pretty hard when my girls were young. And it wasn't easy. But I did it so they could ultimately be more independent.

Because when we don't teach our kids to be independent and to take ownership of the things in their little world (things like their toys and their clothes and their room), then they become entitled. And those kinds of kids are gross. I'm sorry, but they are. They expect everything to be done for them and they complain when it's not.

I used to see those types of kids every day when I taught in the classroom—kids like this one little girl who never liked to clean up her workspace after we did an activity. Religiously, she'd finish her little cutting or gluing project and just get up from the table and walk away, leaving her work area a total disaster and expecting the other kids working at the table to clean up after her.

I remember the first time she did it, too. I called her over to clean up her mess and she just looked at me and said, "But why? They're doing it for me," pointing at the other kids around the table. It wasn't until I asked her what she did when she was at home and made a mess that I figured it out . . . her mom was always cleaning up after her. And there it was: she wasn't being held accountable.

Our kids need to be kids, above all. They work hard when they're young, even though it's a different type of work and a different sort of pace. And we need to remember that. That's why it can be tricky for us to know how much responsibility to put on them and when. Especially since school and sleep and downtime are such priorities. Like I've said, kids can bear more weight than we realize, *than they realize*. Most importantly, they almost always rise to the occasion, whatever that occasion is. Which means we need to challenge them, even early on. Because if we don't, then they won't have the desire to challenge themselves. And you'll end up with a twenty-seven-year-old deadbeat for a kid living in your basement. Not cool. By challenging them early and often, though, you'll end up with a loving, caring kid who can take care of you in your retirement. Winning.

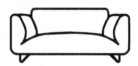

From the Couch of
Debra Fox Gansenberg MSW, LICSW

Gen Z is known as the *Entitlement Generation*. As parents, we must work hard to prevent our children from developing a sense of entitlement or unrealistic expectations.

Kids growing up from generation to generation are often influenced by what's going on in the world, the economy, politics, and the newest gadget or addition to the World Wide Web. As parents, we need to remember it is people in our children's lives, things they do, and places they go that all influence who they will become. It is up to us parents to teach and locate influential people, places, and things to do that will ward of the chances of being spoiled.

Tip: We can begin with teaching our children that "no" is an option. Parents are so afraid to have to deal with a child's response and *no behavior* that they avoid it at all costs, including the lesson that must be taught: you might not always get what you want, that's life. And if you really want "it" you might have to work for it. Lack of interest and motivation to work to earn something are hazards of being handed everything, which is this generation's challenge. Parents, keep your money in your pocket and stop with the handouts. Help kids learn that hard work can lead to good and lasting things.

Tip: Model behavior and responses that you are looking for from your kids. Entitlement didn't come out of thin air, it came from us, the parents who cannot tolerate watching their kid fail or have to work hard. If you demonstrate what good work ethic and dedication look like, your chances of producing a child with the same work ethic is greater. Parents need to step aside and let their child watch, learn, and then see how it feels to do the actual work. Kids need to learn that getting what you want best comes from their own hard work instead of a handout.

Eliminate the power struggle by asking questions about why your child might be pushing back.

Tip: As a parent, when you are told to do something by a boss, parent, or colleague, how does it land on you, are you quick to do what you are told? How would it feel if you were asked respectfully or even requested? Would you feel more apt to proceed? Think of your child. How you frame an expectation is crucial. Put the demands and have-to attitude aside and articulate your request with a respectful manner and kind words, you might be surprised at how your kids respond.

Tip: When you are met with resistance or refusal what is it your child wants you to know? Inquire, ask your child what comes up for him when you make a request. Turn this power struggle into more of a dialogue to better understand the thought process of your child. Once you have gained some insight, ask your child what he might need in order to do what's being asked of him. Sometimes a child might need a little help, better directions, or a little time before he gets started.

Parents, finding your patience, adjusting your expectations, and letting go are the keys to raising self-sufficient children.

Tip: I was taught early on that what we do as a parent sets the precedent for what we will do moving forward. If you are always going to fold your children's laundry, they will always expect that you will until YOU hand over the laundry, teach them how to fold, allow them to practice and *not be perfect*, and then allow them to do this for themselves moving forward. It is hard work to be satisfied with the idea of them taking on such an important job, yet it is imperative to the process of learning and becoming self-sufficient.

Tip: Homework is for your kids to do, not you! The process is typically to assist as a tool in their learning as they master a skill. If you are the one doing the work, then you are the one mastering the skill and the teachers will not know the real skill level of your child. As a parent, our job is to set our children up in order to eventually learn how to tackle things all on their own. Step in by teaching them how to set up a space, organize their time, and check their own work—all great ways to become self-reliant without you giving them the answers or writing their sentences.

Message: As parents, we want our children to be happy, healthy, and successful. One way we can ensure this can happen is to back up, let them do things for themselves and learn what hard work feels like. By creating space for them to become more self-sufficient, they will gain confidence that they indeed can take care of all sort of things. If you are always part of their solution, then they will always need you to be involved. Becoming independent is something they need to be to feel successful, so give them the chance to try it out.

Get Cozy with the Word "No"

It doesn't feel great saying "No" to our kids, but it's important for kids to hear it sometimes.

From the time our kids are little, they want what other kids around them have. No big surprise there, I'm sure. And the last word in the English language that they ever seem to accept is *No*.

As soon as they learn how to pilot their chubby little hands, they're reaching for everything. They're grabbing toys away from their friends, throwing fits, and whining their heads off for us to get them the toy from the TV commercial or the bag of chips from the endcap of the supermarket aisle. The whining evolves very quickly into grunting for those things, which develops even quicker into flat-out demanding them, sometimes to the point where it feels like their first real words are *I want*. And even though that never really ends (sorry), they do usually develop a little perspective once they're older and more mature (I say again, usually). It's the time in between that's the tricky part.

It's when our kids are young that we have to get really comfortable using the word *no*. Like really, really comfortable. Because if we don't pump those brakes early, we run the risk of sliding, headfirst, into a world of spoiled brattiness. And I feel pretty confident none of us wants to be there.

Now why is it that kids always want the stuff other kids have? And why can't they ever take "no" for an answer? (Rhetorical questions, I know.) The answers are pretty obvious: it's because somebody else has it, and they're just not capable of understanding much of anything yet in the way of real limits.

We see it in playgroups, during playdates, and with brothers and sisters. It's a constant issue when our kids are young, an issue that causes huge amounts of stress and anxiety for us and for them. And even though most of us do everything in our power to reason with our kids when they just *have* to have something, a five- or six-year-old has little to no capacity for sustained rational behavior. So reasoning with them is basically pointless. But you can at least establish a pattern: kid wants something, you say "no" to most of the extras—the stuff they don't need even though Susie has it. Basically you say "no" A LOT. Just know that even though you say "no" doesn't mean they'll ask less frequently, they'll just get better at handling it when you do say it. Of course, whenever it makes sense to say "yes," let them enjoy the moment.

Over the years, I've watched little kids go at it with their parents in every public place you can think of, arguing with them because they were just handed a clear and decisive "no." The problem was, after time, the parents caved because the kid was unrelenting. But I'm sorry, *we're* the parents. We're the ones who are supposed to have the mental toughness to handle a whiney seven-year-old. 'Cause you know, they're seven and we still have the ability, as long as we're taller, to pick them up and get them the hell out of Dodge. Zero tolerance; that's the policy we all have to enforce.

We're the ones who are supposed to have the mental toughness to handle a whiney seven-year-old.

Does zero tolerance really work? Sometimes there is more to a process than just saying "no."

In our family, Dave and I have always made it clear to our girls that they'd never get what they were after if they ever publicly threw a fit over something they wanted. Once they were old enough to have legitimate conversations with us, we knew they were old enough to absorb what would happen if they ever acted that spoiled around other people. They'd be extracted from the situation before they had the chance to blink. Oh yeah, and we also used to remind them that if they acted badly around other people, we'd be embarrassing them the first chance we got. You know, mortification disguised as a teachable moment.

Our Kids Don't Need Everything They Lay Their Eyes On

Here's the thing: if someone else has something sparkly or blinky or pretty or cool-looking, our kids want it. Since the beginning of time, people—especially kids—have coveted what other people have. And in most cases, the average little kid will see absolutely no reason why they can't have the Tonka truck or the Presidential Barbie doll. So it takes a reeeeeeally long time and a lot of effort on our part to change that thinking. But it *is* possible. We just need to resign ourselves, up front, that it's going to be an exhausting battle and we're going to take a lot of direct hits to the metaphorical groin before it's over.

Working around kids for so long, I constantly see kids who are rarely, if ever, denied anything by their parents. And believe me, it's nasty looking. You've seen them at the mall or in the supermarket or at the park; the kids who throw fits whenever they don't get what they want. Well, they're behaving that way because they're probably used to getting everything they ask for at home. So they just naturally assume that life functions that way outside the house too. Okay, maybe not the little kids who are still learning to comprehend what *no* means, but when you see a grammar-school-age kid throwing a hissy in the candy store, because he just won't leave without the baseball-size jawbreaker, that's a problem. A problem that's got to be nipped in the ol' bud before it gets out of control.

The other thing to keep in mind is that the earlier we teach our kids to be satisfied and content with what they have, the easier it is for us on the back end as they get older and want fancier and more expensive things.

The earlier we teach our kids to be satisfied and content with what they have, the easier it is for us on the back end.

Remember, the more they grow, the more in tune our kids become with what everyone around them has. They start paying very acute attention to what their friends are wearing and playing with and getting to do. That's because they're moving further out in the world and they're getting exposed to more and more of what the world has to offer. Especially in the way of stuff.

When my girls were in the early elementary school grades, they were no different than any of the other kids. They'd come home daily asking for things in spite of our best efforts to teach them to be content. Even though they weren't asking for things like toys every day—maybe it was just ice cream or candy or to go to the movies—there'd always be some kind of *ask*. And the older they got, the bigger the ask became.

Trust me, we've cycled through all the fads of the month, like the black athletic tube socks that they both *just had to have*, the iPhones, the Ugg boots, the North Face fleeces, the Razor scooters, the Nintendo DSs. Every generation has their own trends, and even though the stuff itself might be different, their desire for whatever the white-hot thing is at the moment is still insatiable.

And the wanting isn't just relegated to physical stuff. Our kids will also want the intangible things, like the same curfew their friends have or the same TV and gaming time their friends get or a bigger allowance. It never really stops. So it's up to us to teach them to be satisfied with what they have.

Everyone wants. It's just part of how we're all fundamentally wired. I mean, if that weren't the case, the word *covet* would never have been put in the Ten Commandments in the first place. But it's there, and it's there for a reason. Because, technically, according to The Big Guy, we're not supposed want what other people have. Yeah, okay, right. In theory, maybe. But the reality is that we still do, whether we're supposed to or not.

And wanting things can be a pretty useful motivational tool when used selectively with our kids. You know, as incentives. Like having a backyard campout when our kids keep their rooms clean all week. Or getting a little extra computer time when they finish all their homework. Or going bowling with friends if they do all their chores around the house. 'Cause we all know those are things they want. And the great byproduct of offering our kids experiences instead of things as incentives is that it helps kids focus on *doing* things rather than just accumulating more stuff.

> 🛋 **Learning when and how to motivate your child is absolutely key to good parenting.**

You Can Even Say "Yes" from Time to Time

Who doesn't remember those feelings of desperately wanting something when we were kids—that need to have something sooooo badly that we could barely breathe or think about anything else? (Obsession, I believe it's called.) I can remember being so preoccupied when I got something stuck in my head that I became consumed by it, to the point of nauseating both my parents. All kids do it. It's normal.

Case in point: When I was around seven or eight, I vividly remember becoming hyper-aware of the fact that most of my friends had dogs. They had snuggly, cuddly, deliciously sweet built-in playmates 24/7, and I wanted one too. So it didn't take me very long to start campaigning to my parents to get one. And, like most kids with an agenda, I campaigned hard.

In my young and naïve brain, I saw no good reason why we shouldn't have a family dog. I was absolutely sure that I was doing my parents a huge favor by suggesting that we get one. Never mind the fact that my mom was *not* a dog person or that our house was empty during the day because both my parents worked or that our yard wasn't fenced in. I got dog in my head and couldn't get it out.

As a result, I wore my poor parents down to a nub begging and pleading for one every time I opened my mouth. And while I don't remember exactly how long I hounded them, I know it went on for a while, because eventually they gave in. And that's what we do a lot of the time. We give in. Even when we're reluctant. Even when we have buckets full of reasons why we shouldn't. Sometimes we just do. Because, as hard as it is for kids to learn how to accept *no* for an answer, it's just as hard for us to learn how to say it.

That's because parenting isn't an exact science—no aspect of it. It's often really, really hard to know when to say "yes" or to say "no" or when to intervene or to back away. Which is why we all screw up so much of the time. And since most of the choices we make involving our kids are motivated by their happiness and well-being, we sometimes cave and do stuff we know we shouldn't do just because we love them. Which is exactly why my parents let me have Murphy.

But don't assume that just because I ended up with a dog that I got everything I wanted growing up. *Au contraire*. And neither have my kids. My mom and dad said "no" when they had to, and so do we. We learned early the importance of teaching our kids that they can't have everything they want. I'll tell you right now exactly how we learned it—we watched other young kids and their parents very carefully when our kids were growing up.

We paid close attention to the whiners and the push-over parents and made mental notes about the kinds of kids we did and *didn't* want to raise. Because believe me, the spoiled brats of the world stood out like they were dressed in neon with blinking lights all over them—so did their parents. They served as good reminders of what *not* to do. Like how we can't give in to everything our kids ask for, for the simple fact that people need limits. Especially little people.

I mean none of us wants to see our kids sad, let alone to be the reason why they're sad. But the plain and simple fact of life is that we can't always give them what they want. Trust me, it's a terrible idea. Because to raise our kids to believe that they can or should get everything is just giving them unrealistic expectations. Because once they're older, they'll realize pretty quickly that the rest of the world isn't going to accommodate them, even if Mommy and Daddy do.

Raising our kids to believe that they can or should get everything is just giving them unrealistic expectations.

I mean, it's okay to want things, and with kids it's expected. But there *has* to come a point when our kids accept the facts that we're not a black hole filled with hundred-dollar bills, it's unhealthy to get everything they ask for, and, most importantly, they need to learn to get comfortable with disappointment because it's always going to be out there. All these epiphanies take time for kids to absorb. Which means that, until they do, we have to be super-diligent reinforcing it every chance we get.

And we also *have* to have a strategy, like we do with every other teaching point with our kids. We have to get them accustomed to us asserting ourselves as their parents. Even though we're the ones they go to for love and support and reassurance, we have to remember that we're still the long arm of the law in our family. Because as much as they need us to be all of those things, they need us to set limits and enforce them. And we've got to be consistent. How they react to the limits we set is on them. When they start crying or throwing stuff or arguing with us, that's on them. When they try to manipulate us to get what they want, that's on them.

To Hold the Line or Flex?

The way we teach this concept is the exact same way we teach every concept to our kids. We hammer it over and over and over again. Then we hold the line tight with both hands and we don't let go. (Okay, maybe we loosen our grip once in a while, but not more than that.) Because even though we're the ones who really need to stick to the rules we make, we are allowed to bend them from time to time. It's called being flexible and making situational decisions. Like if our kids are bugging us to stay up an extra hour and we say "no," and then they bug us some more and we still say "no," we reserve the right to make a compromise. We can say ten more minutes, and they can either be okay with it or go to bed. Giving in to our kids and what they want really only does one thing . . . it reinforces that they're entitled to whatever they're trying to get. And that's the last thing we wanna do, so make those exceptions few and far between.

Also important here is the truth that our kids model how we act around them. If we have outbursts, it's likely they'll do the same. If we're calm the majority of the time when we're dealing with them and their endless requests, then chances are good they'll pick up on our vibe—eventually.

We all know it's hard to stay that course when we've heard the same requests for stuff over and over. It wears us down. Yet when we lay it down with our kids and then just walk away, it's almost always a better outcome than getting into a debate with a raging six-year-old about why they can't have the Barbie camper that their best friend has. I've said "no" to my kids and then let myself go 'round and 'round with them when they pushed back, but the times that I laid it down and just left the room—those were the most successful.

The big mistake a lot of us make over and over is trying to calmly reason with a kid who's been alive for as many years as we have fingers on one hand. It. Doesn't. Work. Like when my girls were finally old enough to sit in the front seat of the car and they automatically assumed that they had control over the radio. They'd ask to listen to whatever the hot pop station was and most of the time I'd say "yes." But not when anything from the '80s came on. Then I'd say "no." Because those were my jams, and I wasn't about to give up the chance to get my groove on to the stuff I listened to as a kid. But, inevitably, I'd get some kind of attitude. To which I'd sometimes respond by snapping at them that I'm just as entitled to choosing what we listen to as they are. I mean, I'm the one who owns the dang car. But that was like lighting a stick of dynamite. Predictably, that would cause an exchange. And not the good kind. Blood would boil (usually mine), and someone's bottom lip would come out. Then verbal punches were thrown. Not effective.

What almost always worked is when I gave the ultimatum that we either listen to "Come on Eileen" without anyone complaining, or the radio goes off and we live in silence. And when I'd hear so much as an odd-sounding sniff from one of them, I'd smack that power button off and just smile. Worked like a charm.

The moral here is that we're the authoritarians. Period. And it's their job to come to terms with that in their own way and at their own speed. This doesn't mean we can't play *Let's Make a Deal* once in a while. I'll let you listen to that song if you promise to clean all the dinner dishes can be a win-win too.

📖 **If your five-year-old is negotiating his bed time, it's time to put him to bed!**

You've Got to Model It

One other thing that really helps our kids absorb that no means no and that limits are actually a good thing is when we, ourselves, model that in our own lives. Especially when we do it around our kids.

📖 **One other thing that really helps our kids absorb that no means no and that limits are actually a good thing is when we, ourselves, model that in our own lives.**

Sure, we're the income-earning grown-ups who can, in theory, buy whatever stuff we want without needing to give anyone an explanation. But when our kids are young and we're teaching them that we can't have everything we want, we need to consciously rein ourselves in to prove the point. Buying whatever we want for ourselves sends a slightly hypocritical message to our kids. So if we practice what we preach, modeling goes a long, long way to proving that argument.

I know it's super tempting sometimes just to give in and give our kids what they want, but it's honestly one of the worst parenting mistakes we can ever make. Ever. Because once we bleed our hand and show them that they do actually have the power to manipulate us, they'll use that power to their advantage every chance they get. It's a classic good-versus-evil dilemma.

As the grown-ups, we all desperately want to keep the peace and sometimes that urge makes us do crazy things, just like wanting the hottest new toy can make our kids go mental and behave like irrational lunatics. How many times have we put the Disney movie on one more time just to avoid the meltdown so we could make our three o'clock conference call without having a wild animal screaming at us in the background? Or shoved the extra handful of Halloween candy in our kid's face just to ensure that the last twenty miles of the five-hundred-mile road trip were in silence? Or told them they could sleep over at their friend's house just because we weren't in the mood for the argument?

I've done it. You've done it. We've all had those frantic moments when we just needed to make them stop. So we can't beat ourselves up too badly when they happen. We just need to try to keep the win column fuller than the loss column. That's not tough to do as long as we stay committed to standing our ground. Because it's the kids who ultimately realize that they can't always get their way who are the ones who'll be able to handle disappointment later in life. Guaranteed.

From the Couch of
Debra Fox Gansenberg MSW, LICSW

Does zero-tolerance really work? Sometimes there is more to a process than just saying no.

When someone says "zero tolerance," do they really mean "I am not going to put up with this sort of behavior anymore!"? Schools, colleges, work places, et cetera, are implementing these policies in order to protect their students and employees from dangerous behavior and others' poor judgement. Our society as a whole has been impacted for the last decade by several incidents that have caused the zero tolerance policy to be developed. Is it really necessary in the home?

Tip: A zero tolerance policy can actually prevent necessary conversations from happening in the home. For instance, if your child uses harmful language towards another family member, slow it down and instead of going from calm, cool, and collected to off the charts upset, create an opportunity to discuss how words impact siblings, as well as what the words really mean. Kids often repeat things they have heard without actually knowing what they mean and then end up reusing them in an inappropriate way or time. If the behavior repeats itself, then preparing a consequence may be the next step.

Tip: Oftentimes a child's intent and what they are actually doing are two very different things. When zero tolerance policy is in place, it will not take a child's age or development into consideration. It is important that when your child does something that you find intolerable, you need to first check in with your own parts and try and understand what is so undesirable about what has been said or done. Then take the time to fit the crime with an appropriate consequence. Zero tolerance really doesn't allow for any space to stop and think and consider all aspects of what has occurred, so we can make an educated decision about a consequence.

Tip: There is an exception to the rule of zero tolerance; can you guess what it is? Yes, if someone is harmful to themselves or someone else you must pull out the zero-tolerance card. Whether you are in a school, home, or office, everyone deserves to be safe and feel safe. If someone in your home is creating a sense of danger or harm you must make it your priority to protect your children, even if it is coming from another child in the home. If you ever feel someone in your home is unsafe, as a parent it is our job to protect them and those around them. Access help to assist with all parties involved.

Learning when and how to motivate your child is absolutely key to good parenting.

Stop and think about what actually motivates you. Is it an incentive plan at work, is it a good review, or is it the potential of losing your job due to poor work performance? Each of us operates differently. The key to getting your child to be motivated to do well in school, behave, or clean up his room is important to the outcome and success.

Tip: What works today might not always work tomorrow. When it comes to figuring out how your child is wired, it can get pretty tricky. Learning how your child is motivated is a challenge, but take notice when your child earns a reward or when your child earns a punishment. Which one tends to be more impactful or meaningful to him/her? For example, "Ruth, I asked you to pick up your room. If I have to ask you again you will lose a token out of your jar." or "Ruth, I am asking you to pick up your room. This is the first time; if you can get it done in the next ten minutes, you will earn a token to put in your jar." Take notice so that moving forward you can do what works best for them. Keep in mind you might need to mix it up to keep them on their toes!

Tip: If your child can't seem to muster up *any* motivation at all, it might be an indication that they aren't working hard enough. Do they get whatever they want, whether it is time on the iPad or television? Did Mimi already get the new Pokémon cards that just came out and drop them off? Did Jake cry and tantrum in Target until he got the Nerf gun he wanted? Stop and think about how you, as parents, manage rewards and punishments. If you can't figure out what is going to work as a reward or punishment, then you might need to reassess how your kid's privileges are being managed. TV, screen time, and a new Lego set are all privileges. A child can't get excited or motivated about something if it is not special.

If your five-year-old is negotiating his bed time, it's time to put him to bed!

The job of a child is to find his/her way. A teen's job is to test along the way. Children must learn when they can go and when they must stop; when it is enough and when they can do more. How do they learn? We are the ones that need to teach them as toddlers, teenagers, and young adults. When is bedtime? It is not up to your five-year-old, it is up to you! Know the difference between negotiating and compromising—it might help you lead the way and set the rules instead of being manipulated by your child.

Tip: Parents often are compelled to compromise in order to feel like there is a fair way around asking kids to stop or start doing something. If a child is asked to go take a shower, it is not unusual to be asked if it can take place at a later time. There is a compromise that then might take place, the giving and taking of ideas, thoughts, or opinions. "Yes, you may take a shower after dinner if you promise to wash your hair too." However, a negotiation is a time when you can actually walk away and have the right to refusal and say "NO." When a child asks, "Mom, can I take my shower later?", Mom is able to say, "This is not up for negotiation; take your shower now, please." As a parent it is a tricky job, but you need to determine whether it is something you are willing to compromise on or if it is not up for negotiation. Knowing this ahead of time will assist in the ease and outcome of your interactions.

Tip: When it comes to drawing the line in the sand and deciding if it's appropriate to compromise, one must look closely at the age and developmental stage of your child. Remember, you are the one teaching the limits and rules. If you are not consistent and concise, they will never learn or really understand the dos and don'ts. Carefully look at the situation to determine if your child needs the reinforcement of the "NO" or if indeed this is a situation where there is some wiggle room. Ultimately, you can tell if you are not doing a good job at this. If you do not see your child understanding or adhering to the house rules, you may want to take a careful look at how often and when you are compromising. You might need to do a better job assessing if this really is a good time to negotiate. In other words, it may be time to keep things simple and stop allowing children negotiating power too often.

Survival Tip 6:

Give Your Kids Free Time to Decompress and Just Be Kids

Let your kids watch TV or play video games or just be—every day . . . or they'll explode.

Back in the day when we were kids, we went to school, maybe we played an instrument, and, if you were like me, you were one of only two girls in your town who played youth baseball. Besides that we played outside until someone's mom blew a slide whistle at sundown that signaled us all to go home. After dinner we played Barbie or Matchbox cars or read actual books or maybe did Mad Libs. Then we called it a day. And that was the way of the world. Now though, our kids are racing from group to club to team to rehearsal, eating dinner on their lap in the car, and every parent is secretly praying for a monsoon to come so practice will be canceled.

Now that your kids are in school, you need to get used to the idea of them doing an awful lot more than just going back and forth to their classroom every day. Now so many kids are coming home from school and pulling on shin guards and karate uniforms and reaching for ballet slippers—all in the same day. While it's great to see our kids busy and engaged and spending their time productively, they still need time to just be kids. Because without that, they're missing some real fundamentals of being young—stuff that we don't always realize they're missing until we're forced to focus on it.

Without the ability to relax and decompress in an unstructured way, our kids have no outlets for relieving stress or anxiety, or solving problems, and they become conditioned to look to us to fill all their time. And when we can't, or we're not available, they're lost.

Because I'm such a visual person, let's take a quick peek at the list I just pulled together of what I think our kids are missing when they're shuttling from activity to activity without any downtime.

- Learning how to entertain themselves
- Quieter, more solitary activities, like curling up with a good book or drawing
- Time to create
- The chance to just daydream
- The opportunity to decompress and process what they're exposed to every day
- The chance to be inspired
- True independence

When we don't give our kids the freedom to explore and be creative and rely on themselves to occupy at least a little of their time, we're setting them up to be co-dependent little robots who just cycle from activity to activity and can't think or entertain themselves on their own.

Put That Parent Guilt to Rest

Our kids still need downtime and free playtime and freedom to make their own choices, in spite of the fact that most parents today feel ridiculous guilt over seeing their kids without anything to do—even for a minute. I know I have. Probably because I, myself, prefer to be busy and productive as a rule. Then again, I'm a grown up. And I also appreciate my quiet time to do nothing. But kids aren't that evolved yet. They do need their time to be structured. Just not all of it. Which is exactly why we need to teach our kids that it's okay to do nothing once in a while—it's okay for them to shut off their brains for a little while. In fact, it's necessary.

"There is a myth that doing nothing is wasting time, when it's actually extremely productive and essential," says Kathy Hirsh-Pasek, PhD, co-author of *Einstein Never Used Flashcards: How Our Children Really*

Learn and Why They Need to Play More and Memorize Less. "During empty hours, kids explore the world at their own pace, develop their own unique set of interests and indulge in the sort of fantasy play that will help them figure out how to create their own happiness, handle problems with others on their own, and sensibly manage their own time. That's a critical life skill."[7]

'Cause in case you haven't heard of it yet, there's this very real and damaging thing called *oversaturation*. In simple terms, it's when we, the parents, sign our kids up for every possible activity and fill every free second of our kid's day to ensure that they have no idle time. As a result, our kids are waaaay overstimulated and they burn out. Fast. And ugly.

> 🛋 **Sometimes individuals are more productive the busier they are; however, kids might be so busy they don't do anything well. There can be benefits to having free time with nothing structured to do.**

In my own experience, saturating our kids with too many activities is bad for the simple reason that, without any downtime to unwind, our kids have no time to decompress and process. It's like bleeding an old-fashioned radiator from the buildup of hot air so it doesn't explode. Well our kids are like mini radiators who need to be allowed to vent to maintain balance in their little systems.

I've had countless conversations with other parents about how lost their kids are when they have even a little bit of free time. And I've had similar conversations with the kids themselves. I used to see kids dragging into school every morning, exhausted and frazzled from being in the car all weekend, traveling from field to field or court to court or practice to practice, and they hated it. Even though they loved the activity they were doing, they resented the fact that they were doing it all the time, which left them with little or no time to do anything else. That constant, unrelenting pace inevitably led to a big crash and an even bigger burn.

I vividly remember one conversation I had with a kindergarten parent in my class after her daughter's full-on meltdown one Monday morning. Her daughter hadn't even made it out of the car at drop-off and she was already throwing a complete nutty. She refused to unbuckle her seat belt and was swatting at her mom every time her mother reached for the buckle. Once her mom finally got the girl out of the car, the walk across the parking lot was equally as rough. The girl refused to walk. Just sat right down on the edge of the grass, crossed her arms and legs and became dead weight. It was like she was at a sit-in for a No-Nukes rally back in the '70s. It took a guidance counselor and her classroom teacher to convince her to come in the building. According to Mom, she had spent the weekend at a travel soccer tournament with three dance recitals squished in between (one full dress rehearsal and two performances). Oh yeah, and she also had two lacrosse games 'cause she was on that team too. The kid was fried.

Sound at all familiar?

So the question becomes: Are we raising a generation of over-achievers and Rhodes Scholars and future pro athletes, or a bunch of frazzled overcommitted overachievers? I think we all know the answer.

The mentality today, at least among the parents I've seen in the school system and the parents I know personally, is to fill every free second of our kids' days with enough stimulation to ensure that they're equal to or ahead of their peers both academically and extracurricu-larly. I see it every day. First- or second- or third-grade kids coming out of their parent's car in the drop-off line lugging backpacks filled with tennis racquets, cleats tied onto the outside, carrying a lacrosse stick in one hand and a trumpet case in the other—poor guys could barely get through the front door of the school. And it doesn't let up in middle school either because on top of everything else, kids are also dealing with hormones. And we all remember how charming those can be.

I can't tell you how many of my friends' kids, or the kids I taught in the classroom, were so overcommitted that they barely knew their own names at the end of every day. They were completely strung out between travel soccer teams and swim teams and piano lessons and cooking classes that they were all frantically rushing back and forth from practice to rehearsal to practice. And you know what that kind of pace does? It creates tense, anxious parents! So while being involved in all of these groups and teams and clubs definitely kept the kids engaged, it also wore them (and their parents) down to little nubs.

I mean, don't get me wrong, I'm all for exposing kids to everything that's around them in terms of athletics and fine arts and languages and music and groups and clubs. Kids need to try on as many hats as they can while they're young to figure out what they like and what they don't like. (Okay, maybe not hats because of the lice thing. Eww.) But there comes a point when we have to pick and choose. We have to do it as parents, and we have to teach our kids how to do it for themselves. Because even though we may be inclined to sign our kids up for every club or team we can find, that will not be healthy for our kids or for us.

Even though we may be inclined to sign our kids up for every club or team we can find, that will not be healthy for our kids or for us.

Just say "No"

These are times when you can practice Survival Tip 5: Get Cozy with the Word "No." It's actually okay to say no to too many activities. In fact, it's necessary. It's on us to be the voice of reason when it comes to how our kids are spending their time. In the same way that we shouldn't be forcing them to be a lacrosse player or a flautist, we also shouldn't let them join three different sports teams when they're seven. We need to be actively setting limits for our kids, not just with things like bedtimes and the amount of time they spend in front of the TV and the food they're eating, but also with the kinds of commitments they make at a young age.

I know it's easy to get hung up on not wanting to disappoint our kids. Every parent wants to be popular with their children. But learning when to say no is way more important than being popular. We have to be the ones who keep our kids and their schedules in check. And it's tough, because our kids are seeing their friends playing on multiple teams and involved with Girl Scouts and drama clubs and hip-hop classes and they want in. Why? Because they don't want to miss out. We often overextend ourselves, too, because we don't want to be left out either. We're seeing all the other moms and dads standing in line with their registration forms and feeling like we're doing our kids a disservice by not signing them up too. In truth, we're idiots. Our kids need a break from responsibility just as much as we do.

Learning when to say no is way more important than being popular. We have to be the ones who keep our kids and their schedules in check.

Ironically, the American Academy of Pediatrics says to "delay sports specialization until at least age fifteen to sixteen to minimize risks of overuse injury."[8] They've got too many growing and developing tendons and ligaments that can be compromised by excessive overuse. So I guess that means that kids should be playing sports at the elementary level for, uh, fun. Because when young kids cross over from playing recreational sports, which are designed to move their bodies and give them a sense of being part of a team and a feel for sportsmanship, into the realm of super-competitive sports, that's where the problems start. It's when too much pressure to perform is put on young kids that they cave.

So do we want our kids to learn the feeling of being part of a team or a group or a club? Absolutely. Being part of something bigger than ourselves is an essential part of growing up. It speaks to teamwork and collaboration and flexibility, and it teaches us how to communicate and does amazing things for building self-esteem. Plus, it helps us learn how to build relationships. All invaluable lessons. But knowing when enough is enough for our kids is on us. Saying no to the third travel field hockey team is on us. Teaching our kids that quality is more important than quantity is on us.

> 🛋 **One of the best lessons one can learn is that we can lead a life where less is more in all aspects of our daily living.**

Encouraging them to stop and step away from the grind and just chill is on us. Because when our kids have free time to rest and reset and recharge, that's when the magic happens. That's when they learn to embrace being bored and think on their own and entertain their brains and invent themselves. So if you really want to help your kids become well-rounded adults, give them enough downtime to balance the uptime. Not only will they thank you for it, but they'll be calmer and less stressed because of it. And so will you.

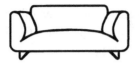

From the Couch of
Debra Fox Gansenberg MSW, LICSW

Sometimes individuals are more productive the busier they are; however, kids might be so busy they don't do anything well. There can be benefits to having free time with nothing structured to do.

Our society today is fast-paced and all about efficiency. Use every minute of every day doing something that will lead to a productive outcome is the mindset. The mistake here is that the outcome has to be something tangible or measurable. Our society needs to stop and understand that sometimes the most invaluable things are time and space, which really is not anything we can actually see. However, we can experience in ourselves the benefits of creating time and space to regroup and repair. Try it at home, it might be more valuable than you think. Less tantrums and meltdowns, less reactivity, and less misbehavior are all benefits of taking time to slow down and recharge.

Tip: A side effect of a plugged-in and constant contact generation is the idea that they are in constant motion and oversaturated in updates, pictures, and tweets. A hazard for our young Gen Zers is the fact that they do not have any other reference to relaxing other than having a phone in hand while they are sprawled out on the couch or even using the bathroom. As a parent it is our job to help kids learn how to manage their time and space. Gen Zers might benefit from starting with the concept of unplugging. Hard to believe that relaxing and unwinding could include empty hands and a good book or listening to music. Parents, set them up, talk the talk and walk the walk. Set good examples as well as clear limits around when enough is enough.

Tip: As adults we are tangled up in the busy web of life and oftentimes we make it busier by doing everything we *think* everyone else is doing. Playdates, travel teams, music lessons, religious school, and socializing. Each family is different and made up of so many variables: work schedules, health needs, learning challenges, and other commitments. As a parent you need to check in with what YOUR family needs, not what everyone else seems to be doing. Set appropriate time aside for what it takes your child to complete homework without rushing out the door to practice. Be realistic about whether or not you and your child can handle more than one sport in a season, especially if there are multiple children in a family. On the weekends it might be important to stay engaged with a certain group of friends; however, maybe you need to skip the family get-togethers because it throws your children off their eating and sleeping schedules and, as a result, impacts the bigger picture during the school week.

One of the best lessons one can learn is that we can lead a life where less is more in all aspects of our daily living.
Sometimes we can get caught up in having lots of things or having lots of friends. How would it be to really live a fulfilling life where it is about quality and not quantity? Kids only need one good friend to walk into the schoolyard with. Your son only needs one pair of sneakers until he outgrows them. Your daughter only needs one versatile phone case that can match with all her outfits. As a generation, these kids seek out quantity over quality often due to their overindulged upbringing. We can work to prevent this from happening by making simple changes to our decision-making process.

Tip: As parents, we need to lead by example here. Limit your wants and must haves to needs. Kids are watching what their parents do. If you attend every social function you are invited to, they will want to do the same. Explain to them that you are choosing to stay at home Saturday night to spend quality time together and relax instead of going out to dinner with a friend. When you are headed to the store and you need a new belt because yours doesn't fit anymore, explain what you are doing and go in looking for that specific item and leave with the belt instead of walking out with a cart full of stuff.

Tip: As a society, we spend time trying to get it all done: homework, office work, returning emails or phone calls. What would it be like if we gave that much time and attention to ourselves and our loved ones? Work in time for emotional intimacy as a family. Instead of filling up your calendar with social commitments with others, what would be like to fit in quiet time or family time? Parents, it is your responsibility to create opportunity for quiet time and connection. Create a family activity or meal and request everyone's presence. By practicing this, you are teaching kids to make downtime a priority both for themselves and their loved ones. They will then learn and love this tradition and work it into their lives as they grow older.

Don't Be Afraid to Give Your Kids Consequences

Kids need boundaries, so you've gotta hold the line.

Kids break rules. It's just what they do. They're wired for it. I mean, it's what *we* all did when we were kids, right? And it's our job as their parents to tame them—a job that takes endless amounts of time, incredible dedication, and a ton of patience. But it *can* be done. I swear.

One way or another, every kid tests limits, pushes boundaries, and tries our patience. I guess you could say it's like a rite of passage. A big part of growing up involves figuring out what you *can* and *can't* get away with. We only need to look as far back as our own childhood for proof that we all do it to one degree or another.

Every Kid Loves to Push Buttons

I mean, how many times did you or your sister or brother push your mom's buttons? Too many to count, I'm sure. And how many times did we get busted by our dad for staying up later than our bedtime? Plenty. And how often did we watch our friends make the dumbest decisions—like putting their hand on the stove burner to see if it was hot—in spite of the fact that they knew it would end badly? Too often, believe it or not.

These things—and *so* many more—happen because kids aren't always that smart. Sorry, but they just aren't. Even though I was a pretty good kid growing up, in terms of following rules, I still did my share of thoughtless, irresponsible things even after my parents gave me pretty clear-cut warnings not to. Things like scooting down a handicapped ramp on my little plastic scooter immediately after my mom said *Do **not** ride anywhere near that ramp because you'll go too fast and won't be able to stop.* Which I ignored, of course. Because, like most little kids, I assumed I was invincible. In my underdeveloped little brain, it never occurred to me that I could lose control and end up flying over the handlebars, landing in a full face-plant on the concrete (chin first). Twelve stitches later . . .

Or, a year later, when my mom asked me to walk cautiously around the stray, historically unfriendly dog in my neighborhood to avoid getting bitten. Which my naïve little intellect translated as code for sneak behind him and pull his tail. More stitches. That poor dog. My poor mom.

My own kids were no different when they were that age, choosing to push our buttons. Like when Libby, my youngest, was around eight, we took a road trip to New York City to visit the American Girl store. It was a dream come true for her. She'd waited weeks to make the trip. Dressed in their best outfits and loaded with every accessory they could carry, all her favorite American Girl dolls came, too. To her, it was the equivalent of going to Disney World. I think we were somewhere around Times Square when her meltdown started. Though I honestly can't remember the exact reason why she lost it, I do remember that it was bad. Like really bad—so bad that Dave and I had to bring out the big guns, leaving us no choice but to issue an ultimatum. *Pull yourself together or we're not going to the American Girl store.*

Well, let's just say it didn't end well. She couldn't get a grip on herself, so it left us no choice. She forced our hand and we had to nix going to American Girl or look like the softest parents on the planet. It was brutal on everyone, but it had to be done in the interests of follow-through. We considered it a teachable moment, a life lesson. And it clearly worked because the impact of us walking past the store and not going in was profound. Libby was devastated. (And so was I. Pretty sure I cried myself to sleep that night in the hotel.) In the end, even though holding that line was beyond tough, it sent a necessary message that bad behavior wouldn't be tolerated without consequences. She heard us loud and clear. The next time she pushed our buttons and put us in a similar situation, we reminded her of that day in New York and the memory hit her hard, right between the eyes. Hard enough to disrupt another outburst.

Consequences Can Work Miracles

When Libby was in middle school, she decided to momentarily become a door-slammer, even though I was *very* clear about what would happen if people slammed doors. She was testing limits, obviously, trying to annoy me because I denied another request to go to the mall. So she let the door fly. To which I issued an ultimatum. *Slam it again and you'll wish you didn't.* You can guess what happened. A flathead screwdriver was all I needed to make my point. Her door lived in the garage for three days. No doors have been slammed since.

I guess what I'm trying to say is that our kids will challenge our authority, our rules, and our advice every single chance they get. And they do that for what feels like a really, really long time. Long enough that you're almost convinced that they'll never outgrow the behavior. In their defense, the reason why kids constantly do and say dumb stuff and have to be disciplined is because they haven't been around long enough to understand the law of *cause* and *effect*. Which is why they're constantly making the same mistakes over and over and over again. To the point when, as the mom and dad, you just want to bash your head against a wall, because they never seem to learn a lesson. Don't panic if you're feeling that way. Because we all feel that way at some point along the line. It takes a long, long time for a child's brain to form all the connections necessary to learn how to reason and think like rational, intelligent people.

> 📖 **Kids are doing their job when they are challenging your rules, pushing the limits, and asking why. Kids will show us that they learn when you least expect it!**

That was the case for one of the girls in my daughter Riley's eighth-grade class who just couldn't seem to respect the No Cell Phones in the Classroom Rule. She kept sneaking onto her phone during class, even though her teacher constantly took away her phone whenever she was caught using it. The problem was the teacher had to give the girl her phone back at the end of every day, so the girl continued to break the rule. It was only when the teacher reached out to the girl's parents with the issue that things changed. Once her parents learned their daughter was abusing the cell phone rule in school, they manned up and confiscated her phone for a full week. Like zero phone for an entire seven days, which, to a middle-school kid, is like the worst consequence imaginable. Her parents also told her that if she was caught with her phone in school again, the length of the consequence would double every time. Needless to say, no one ever saw the girl's phone out at school again. Solid parenting right there.

Now I try never to get too technical, but sometimes it serves a purpose. By understanding *why* something functions the way it does, we better know how to manage it (or, in our case, how to manage *them*). If we have a decent idea of what's going on under the hood, we can better handle ourselves when there's a breakdown.

With that in mind, the scientific explanation for what's going on in your kid's head when they're young and making the same mistakes every four minutes has to do with synapses. In simple terms, synapses are links between two nerve cells, comprising a tiny gap across which impulses pass by diffusion of a neurotransmitter. (I know, I've already gotten too technical. But stay with me.) In English, and very crudely put, synapses help transmit messages around our brains by sending electrical impulses from one neuron to the next, to the next, and so on. Fascinating stuff, actually. And broken down even further: Your kids will keep flipping a nutty over the same stupid stuff until the right connections are made in their little brains. Which will ultimately allow them to stop the behavior that is driving you crazy.

The thing is, the connections get stronger the more our kids use them. In other words, they have to keep screwing up until they learn not to screw up anymore. Then they actually have to practice not screwing up anymore. This all explains why they don't often figure stuff out on the first try. Or the second. Or the thirtieth.

📖 **Identifying a start or stop behavior takes awareness. Teaching and sustaining the new behavior takes time. Be patient, change is a s-l-o-w process.**

Connections get stronger the more our kids use them. They have to keep screwing up until they learn not to screw up anymore.

It is a lot like how muscle tissue develops, actually. We can't build muscle overnight. It's a process. We lift weights, we rest, our muscle fibers break down and then regenerate, and little by little, over time, we get stronger. The same exact process happens when we try to teach our kids how to behave. They make a bad choice, we discipline them or give them a consequence, and little by little they learn and remember what will happen to them if they pull the same stunt again. In other words, we're strengthening their *character*, rather than muscle. Get it?

Like when my friend's fifth-grade son decided he didn't need to read the book his class was reading for their book reports. He just completely blew it off. Didn't even crack the cover. And his parents only found out about the assignment by chance at a parent–teacher conference. They were honest with the teacher and said they knew nothing about the book report and hadn't seen their son doing any reading at home whatsoever. (He was totally busted.) And when they confronted their son, they told him he needed to go straight into school the next day and admit to his teacher that he hadn't read the book and accept whatever consequence the teacher gave out. He did. And of course, aside from the consequence of the embarrassment of admitting to not reading the book, his grade for the project got dinged pretty badly. But, as far as I know, he's never blown off an assignment like that again.

The good thing is, most of the stuff our kids get into when they're young is, like my husband Dave likes to say, pretty vanilla. It's more or less harmless—annoying but harmless.

Set Those Boundaries and Follow Through

In the early years, kids are just too inexperienced at life to realize that when they do or say something that's inappropriate, they're going to get nailed for it by someone. At least most of the time. That, my friends, is where we step in.

As kids, they simply haven't developed the cognitive power to see two seconds beyond where they are at the moment. That means, when they push our buttons or make bad decisions, chances are excellent that they haven't even bothered to think past their words hitting the air. This is that critical point where we have to put our money where our mouth is and hand out consequences: little ones for the little stuff and bigger ones for the bigger stuff. Although, between us, it's not really as much *what* the consequence is as that there *is* one. Which means that the real key to effectively disciplining our kids is disciplining them with some kind of consistency.

It's not really as much *what* the consequence is as that there *is* one.

It's never easy to discipline our kids. No parent wants to bring down the hammer, believe me. God knows I didn't on that day in New York. But it is necessary, both for our kids' well-being and for ours. Kids need boundaries—clear-cut, defined boundaries—that help them differentiate right from wrong. It's that simple. And setting those boundaries is entirely our responsibility.

Think of it another way. What would happen to the new dog you just brought home from the shelter if you let him out in the backyard and the yard didn't have a fence? Bye-bye doggy. The dog can't be expected to set its own boundaries. Dogs don't do that—and neither do our kids.

According to ResponsiveClassroom.org, "we need to give our kids logical consequences that are directly related to our kid's behaviors in order to help them fix their mistakes."[9] For instance, when you're giving out consequences, you want to ensure that they're logical and that they corelate to the misbehavior in a way that safeguards the integrity of the child. Keep in mind that it's our kid's behavior that's the issue, not the child. Also, pay attention to your tone of voice as a way of differentiating logical consequences from a full-on punishment. Remember, it's not what you say, but how you say it. Like if you start screaming at your kid to clean up the milk they just spilled, now you're not giving a them a logical consequence anymore; now you're punishing them. Make sure the consequence you're giving out fits the offense. I mean, having your kid mop the floor because they spilt the milk in the kitchen is reasonable, but having your child mop the floor because they pulled their sister's hair is not.

Most of the heavy lifting we do as moms and dads is really just about common sense and backbone, both of which go hand-in-hand when raising kids. Unfortunately, not all parents are born with equal parts common sense and spine. See, whether you're thinking about it this way or not, the truth is, we're all products of who and where we come from, at least to some degree. That means that who our kids become as people is, for the most part, a direct result of how we handle them as kids.

Now I know this seems like an obvious concept, and you're probably wondering why I'm even bothering to bring it up. Well, it just so happens there are way more parents out there than you even realize who give their kids ultimatums and threaten consequences for bad decisions or behavior and then don't follow through at the eleventh hour.

Parents blurt out that TV privileges will be taken away or electronics will be forfeited as consequences, and then they cave once they have to follow through. Everyone hates to be the bad cop when it comes to disciplining our kids. Believe me, I get it. I've been the bad and the good cop, and they're both tricky. When you're the bad guy a few times, the perception of you becomes that you are the bad guy. No parent wants to be typecast as the mean one; but then, if you're the good guy all the time, your kids will steamroll you. Happens every time. They'll play on your sensitivity and what they perceive as your softheartedness, and they'll kick you in the throat every time.

I saw it daily working in school. I watched kids habitually forgetting backpacks and homework and textbooks and backpacks (yeah, amazing, isn't it?) and parents came in swearing up and down that it was the last time they'd bail out their kid. Week in and week out, those same parents stormed into school angry and frustrated at their kids for forgetting things, yet they never gave their daughter the obvious consequence of doing without whatever it was that she forgot. It drove me absolutely nuts.

Sure, as a kindergartener or a second- or third-grader, our kids haven't been exposed to enough of the school routine yet to remember everything, so we cut them some slack until they get into a groove, usually around third or fourth grade. But the overarching rule is still true, even for these little guys, that if they forget their homework or they're misbehaving or not following directions, there needs to be a consequence. In school. At home. Everywhere. And that rule should follow them all the way through middle school and high school and until they're out on their own.

> 🛋 **Believe it or not, our kids are often in the driver's seat; they are in more control than they realize.**

Okay, so even though the word *consequence* usually has a negative connotation, it doesn't always have to be a bad thing. It's like anything: it depends on how you spin it. That's why your goal as a parent shouldn't be to prevent negative behavior (that's just a lost cause), it should actually be on reinforcing positive behavior, which is why we should never be giving our kids **punishments** for their behavior. That's nothing but negative, especially when you consider that a punishment is nothing more than retribution or getting back at someone. And we both know that's no way to raise a kid. A **consequence**, though, is an effect or result of someone's actions. It's super important to understand the difference. Think of my daughter missing the American Girl store (and don't worry, we did that another day when she was ready to behave). Her missing that opportunity was a result of her not behaving in a way that we should behave in the middle of New York City.

What we need to be doing in terms of effectively disciplining our kids boils down to one thing. (Okay, maybe two.) We have to consistently bring down the hammer when our kids need a consequence. And we have to **Hold the line!** at all costs. Which means that we have to use the old Yul Brynner line from the Ten Commandments: *So it is written, so it shall be done.* Once we say it, we have to follow through with it. In fact, that's the only rule that really matters in the end. Because if we don't stand our ground, the enemy (our kids) will breach our defenses. And if our defenses are compromised, we've just lost the war.

So just take a series of deep breaths and resign yourself to doling out and enforcing whatever appropriate consequence is necessary in the moment. Remember, consequences are reminders to our kids of what to do and what not to do. 'Cause in this game, you need to be in it to win it. And if you hold that line when you're establishing boundaries, you'll win way more of the battles than you'll lose.

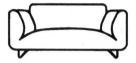

From the Couch of
Debra Fox Gansenberg MSW, LICSW

Kids are doing their job when they are challenging your rules, pushing the limits, and asking why. Kids will show us that they learn when you least expect it!

Tip: Our children are constantly transitioning from one developmental stage to another; however, one of the constants is their need to test limits, question rules, and constantly ask why. Parents, they are doing their job. More importantly, our job is to teach them what they can and cannot do. When you teach them, remember to be clear and concise and keep it simple. Your instructions are very important. The easier the instructions are, the greater the chance your kids will not mess it up.

Tip: If you are repeating yourself than you are doing it right! Kids are smart; they will try and try again with the goal of receiving information from you whether they can or cannot proceed. Remember, they are showing you they do not know or they need another gentle reminder, so you must teach them . . . over and over and over again. Be as pleasant the last time as you are the first time.

Tip: Parents, a mistake we often make is to assume our kids should already know the answer. Read their cues; if they do not do what you have asked, if they did not do it right the first time, or they did something again you already asked them not to do, they are teaching **you** something. It might feel frustrating and almost comical at times, but the truth of the matter is that your child is teaching you that they still require your direction. Calm the part of you that has become impatient and begin again.

Identifying a start or stop behavior takes awareness. Teaching and sustaining the new behavior takes time. Be patient, change is a s-l-o-w process.

Tip: Have you ever worked on a task when you aren't quite sure what is being asked of you? In many cases, our own confusion about what we are asking of our children can make it difficult for them to proceed with a request. It is imperative that you figure out the type of behavior you are actually looking for. Once you have that figured out, your directions will become much clearer and easier to deliver and, as a result, your child has a greater chance at success.

Tip: There are stop behaviors and start behaviors, and understanding the difference is important when making a request of your child. A start behavior would include things like, "Can you please start getting ready for school?" or "Could you get your homework started, please?" These are clear behaviors that you want them to begin to do. A stop behavior is the opposite. "Could you please stop fighting with your sister?" or "I asked you to stop playing your video game and put down the controller." Here you are making it clear that these are actions you want to end. Once you have the type of behavior figured out, then the directive becomes much easier to identify and directions become clearer.

Tip: The process of changing ones' behavior takes time. For instance, you have decided you want your child to start making his bed every day before school. This start behavior might take some time before he/she is doing it on their own and doing it well. First, teach your child by modeling the start behavior and the expectations of the outcome (What should the bed look like when made—we've all seen some interesting results there. Show your child what you want to see.). Second, the next several times watch your child start this new behavior and guide them through your expectations. Give them a couple weeks to do the task and meet the expectation. Third, provide a gentle reminder moving forward that this start behavior is expected. Change can be hard and very slow depending on the task at hand and your child's abilities.

Believe it or not, our kids are often in the driver's seat; they are in more control than they realize.

Tip: Believe it or not, your children have more control than they realize. When setting your child up for success it is important to explain to them that they are in the driver's seat. They have the power to decide whether or not they earn a reward or a punishment. If they follow directions and do it the first time, they could earn a token or sticker for their charts. If they do not choose to follow the directions, they can earn a punishment or consequence. Remember that you just hand the reward or punishment out, they have the power to choose which one they want.

Tip: There are different types of consequences that would be useful to review with your kids. There are natural consequences that actually just happen. For instance, "You didn't study for your test and that is how you earned an F." It is helpful to loop around and explain that they earned the F by not studying, which was their choice! Another type of consequence is a positive one, or what we might see as a reward. In this case they chose to study for their test and earned a B, a positive outcome rewarded by a good choice to study. Then there is the negative consequence or more often referred to as the punishment. In this case, when requesting a stop behavior, "Please don't run out in the street, there is a car coming!" and your child continues to run out to chase his ball, he will earn a punishment. Your child is headed to a time-out because he chose not to listen and proceed out in the street anyway. Remind him/her that he earned the time out when he chose not to follow directions, a choice he made.

Tip: A common challenge for many parents is the child who has not quite developed good self-management skills along the way. As our children develop, our hope is that their self-control is something that matures and that they use consistently. The dilemma for many parents is factoring in a child that might have a deficit in this area. There are many children who might have a learning challenge or disorder that causes him/her a delay or inconsistent ability to use good self-management. In this case, enlisting help for the child and support for the parents will assist in the added challenges to the parenting process. Don't get discouraged, you and your child are not alone, there are many kids that fall into this category in our world today. Seek out resources and a good support system and it will make your journey more pleasant and hopefully more successful too.

Survival Tip 8:

Learn to Let Go

**You don't need to cut the cord altogether,
but you do need to give your kids enough slack
to help them grow**

Now I'm not suggesting that your grade-schooler open a checking account and start renting a loft apartment in the next town. We're not there yet, don't worry. Most little kids barely know how to tie their own shoes. They're just little peanuts, and they're only standing on the outermost edge of their first taste of independence as they head off to school for the first time.

What you need to remember is that baby steps become big strides quicker than you can imagine. So if you're still holding their hand when they should be standing on their own two feet, you run the giant risk of raising a kid who can't think for herself. Because then, to be blunt, you're screwed. And so are they.

This all really ties into all that responsibility training that we talked about earlier. Start teaching them life skills early. Even when our kids are young, they're much more capable of taking care of themselves than we think they are. They're little copycats who just want to mimic and do the things we do. The more our kids get to do by themselves, the more they'll start to rely on themselves instead of us. Invest the time in teaching them how to get dressed or tie their shoes or make a sandwich or ride a bike, and all of those things will translate to more independence and confidence for them—and more peace of mind for us.

📖 **Kids need opportunities to witness for themselves that they are capable, self-sufficient, and good at something they didn't think they could handle. When you believe in yourself, everything is possible!**

Start with Little Chores

But how do we know when to begin teaching all these little things? It's not easy to predict when our kids are ready to do certain things on their own. That's because each child is unique and hits certain milestones at different times. It's okay to teach a skill and then observe how your child does. They may not be great at making their own bed when they're five, but giving them the opportunity to start trying will ensure that they eventually get it. If you try a skill they aren't quite ready for, wait six months and let them try again or choose part of the task that they can do well. Maybe getting the covers pulled up perfectly is too much for them to master at first, but placing the pillow and stuffed animals on after you straighten covers is task they can take pride in.

The more chances we give our kids to think and act for themselves, the more independent they become. The more independent they become, the more self-confident and resilient they are in the long run. (And the sooner you let them pour their own Cheerios on Saturday morning, the more time you're gonna get under the covers on the weekend!)

Here's a good breakdown of age-appropriate chores for your kids from WebMd.com:[10]

Chores for children ages 2 to 7:

- Put toys away
- Fill pet's food dish
- Put clothes in hamper
- Wipe up spills
- Dust
- Pile books and magazines
- Make their bed
- Empty wastebaskets
- Bring in mail or newspaper
- Use hand-held vacuum to pick up crumbs
- Water flowers
- Unload utensils from dishwasher
- Wash plastic dishes at sink
- Fix bowl of cereal
- Sort laundry
- Sweep floors
- Set and clear table
- Help make and pack lunch
- Weed and rake leaves
- Keep bedroom tidy

Chores for children ages 8 to 9:
Any of the above chores and:

- Load dishwasher
- Put away groceries
- Vacuum
- Help make dinner
- Make own snacks
- Wash table after meals
- Put away own laundry
- Sew buttons
- Make own breakfast
- Peel vegetables
- Cook simple foods, such as toast
- Mop floor
- Take pet for a walk

Chores for children ages 10 and above:
Any of the above chores and:

- Unload dishwasher
- Fold laundry
- Clean bathroom
- Wash windows
- Wash car
- Cook simple meals with supervision
- Iron clothes
- Do laundry
- Babysit younger siblings (with adult in the home)
- Clean kitchen
- Change their bed sheets

By encouraging our children to **own** certain responsibilities—even the little ones—we raise them to have a healthy self-esteem. There's no greater feeling to little kids than being able to depend on themselves. But to do that, we need to give our kids responsibilities. Small ones to start, obviously, like clearing their dishes and throwing their dirty clothes in the hamper. By middle school, they are ready to move on to the bigger stuff, like mowing the lawn or cooking dinner. And on and on.

📖 **Though it may be easier to do a job yourself, the cost-benefit of having children do chores is important to consider.**

Let Your Kid Drive the Bus as Often as They Can

When our kids start school, it's the perfect opportunity to start giving them a modest amount of slack to start taking ownership of their little lives. And at this age, that means encouraging them to do the tiny but important things, like starting homework on their own, cleaning up their workspace, and hanging up their own coat. By letting them do these small, yet significant things, we're saying to them, *We know you've got this, honey. We know that you're ready for what lies ahead.* And believe me, it's those tiny acts of independence that jet propel our kids to the next level of autonomy—autonomy that can't be reached if you're hovering over your daughter in the school lobby every morning, keeping her from being independent and branching out to connect with new friends. If you're the one picking out what your son wears every morning, he'll never learn to dress himself.

That autonomy can't be reached if you're like some parents I see three times a week dropping off forgotten water bottles and mittens and homework assignments. Schools! Have! Drinking fountains! No one's going to die of thirst because they don't have their BPA-free water bottle.

Working in the school system for more than a decade, I've seen some pretty outrageous examples of parents who couldn't let go. You know them, the *helicopter parents* who take overprotectiveness to a sickening level. They're constantly by their child's side: carrying their backpack for them or building the shoebox diorama or speaking for them instead of letting their daughter speak for herself. Let me tell you, the only thing that does is raise a kid who can't let go. Whether you realize it yet or not, our kids take their social and emotional cues from us. If they smell fear or sadness on us as we drop them off at school, the chances are good they're going to mimic that same fear and sadness. If they see us idling in the car watching them from the curb, you can bet cash money that they're not going inside without a fight. Because if we're not willing to leave them, they're certainly not going to be willing to leave us.

Do not be like one mom who would actually time her drop-off visits to coincide with when her son's class would be transitioning from the classroom to music or gym or recess. She knew his schedule well enough that she managed to walk into the front lobby at the *exact* time her kid was coming down the hall. It was uncanny, almost like she had some cosmic GPS tracking sensor telling her his exact location. And even though she'd always complain to me that he'd forget his head if it wasn't attached, she'd still bring his sneakers or science binder or lunchbox every single time. Every. Single. Time. And the kid knew it, so there was never a reason for him to take ownership or responsibility. Classic enabling right there.

> 📖 **Natural consequences tend to be the most impactful, because they do not involve anyone trying to manipulate the outcome, it just happens. Providing the appropriate reminder or expectation is fine, but know when to draw the line so your child learns that he/she is responsible for the outcome.**

Trust that if your son gets cold at recess, he'll likely remember his gloves the next time. Your daughter won't flunk out of kindergarten because she left her "Signs of Spring" worksheet at home. When your middle-schooler decides to blow off his part of a group project, that's the time to hang back and let him deal with the consequences of his actions. Let him deal with the fallout of his friends getting angry that their grades suffered because he didn't do his part. Let him explain to his teacher why he's the only one who didn't contribute to the project. Well before they graduate from grade school, our children need to start thinking and acting for themselves. And this is when we start letting them. Because these are the best lessons.

If our kids know *we* believe in them, they'll start believing in themselves. They'll start to think and act independently, because we've given them the confidence to take chances and loosen their grip on Mom and Dad a little. And that's essential. Because, I'm telling you, you don't want to be *that Mom* who walks your son into his first job interview. How do you prepare your child for independence? Use the transition to each new grade as a mile marker for introducing more and more independence to our kids. The start of a new school year is the perfect time to empower them to learn to stand alone (just a little more) as they really start navigating the world around them.

Remember, teaching our kids how to be successful doing everyday tasks builds confidence. It lays the ground work for all of the more complicated, adult stuff that comes later in life, like relationships and managing money and, eventually, a career and their own family. It's these tiny gestures of trust on our part that help put them on the path to becoming independent learners and thinkers. Mastering tasks also creates a sense of pride in being able to do things for themselves. And that motivates kids to want to do more and more on their own. I guess you could call it a domino effect, because one successful accomplishment creates a feeling of pride, and that feeling of pride usually leads to the urge to do more independently, which is *exactly* what you want.

That's why, as hard as it is to do initially, it's vital that we take small opportunities, early on, to let our kids feel what it's like to be separated from us, to depend on other people, and, most importantly, to rely on themselves. And it's just as crucial for us to start the long and painstaking process of loosening our grip. Believe me, it's necessary.

> 🛋 **Our process of family takes on different purposes. If parenting has been done successfully, there is the hope that children will want to spread their wings and fly. Parents need to step aside and create the space for this to happen.**

That Physical Separation Is Rough but Necessary

I know that none of us is ever completely ready to step back and let our kids drive the bus. Especially after being joined at the hip for the first five or so years of their life. Dave and I were petrified when our first daughter went off to school. Watching her walk through that door for the first time, like a little Sherpa carrying all of her own supplies and gear, put a giant lump in both our throats. It's a bittersweet moment for sure.

I remember trying so hard to bite back the tears and stop my bottom lip from twitching just so she didn't catch on to how sad I was to see her go, but inside I was dying. The closer she got to the classroom door, the harder it got for me to hide the thick lump of emotion rising in my throat. For me, it was like a mini life-flashing-before-my-eyes kind of moment.

It was so hard to know what to do that first time, her looking too cute for words dressed in her little denim skirt and red top with her monogrammed big-girl backpack. Did we both walk her up the hill? (Yes, we did.) Did we hold her hand? (Yes, one on either side.) Did I look like a sentimental loser as I cried when she walked through the classroom door? (Yup, did that too.) Would her lunch stay cold? Would she remember how to tie her shoe if it came undone? Would she forget me during those six long hours? I was pathetic. Little did I know that all of my friends were thinking the exact same things.

In that split second that I kissed her good-bye and watched her pair up with another little girl in her class, I saw her as a newborn, then doing her first commando crawl, then as a toddler, then a tiny little person who could zip her own coat and tie her own shoes.

On the walk back to the car, Dave tried to console me while I rattled off a flurry of crazy-mom talk: "Well now what?! Now what am I supposed to do?! She doesn't need me anymore. Did you see all those little girls running up to play with her in the playground? She won't even remember me at pick-up" (heavy sobs). (Side note: hormones make mothers go slightly insane.)

See on the one hand, we know that they're ready to make that transition—ready to start acclimating to life at school. But on the other hand, the idea is terrifying because it means letting go. And no parent wants to do that. We feel if our kids aren't with us we can't protect them, and protecting our kids is our number one responsibility as parents, right? Of course it is, but it's by no means our only responsibility.

Equal to protecting our kids is our job to teach them the skills and give them the knowledge to be able to protect themselves and thrive when they're finally out from under our roof. To do that we need to know when to step in and when to step aside—something that only happens by trial and error. And it doesn't happen overnight. Everyone—parent and child—needs to wade into the water one toe at a time, so we can adjust to the new world around us without being totally shocked and wanting to jump back out of the pool.

Let's face it, we live in a crazy, unpredictable world—a world that's decidedly different from the world we grew up in when we were kids. You remember what it was like when we were kids: People left their front doors open at night and their cars unlocked, and we played outside from sunup to sundown. Our moms and dads wouldn't even know where we were most of the time, sometimes for half the day. Life was simpler. There was no social media threatening the safety and well-being of our kids. No internet predators. No peanut-free lunch tables to consider. There were no school shootings. In a lot of ways, life was less complicated. As the mother of two daughters, I get how scary it is to watch my girls go out into the world. Letting them go means giving up a certain amount of control, and that can be traumatic for parents. But learning to let go also means inspiring our kids to take charge, to take ownership, and to handle adversity—skills that are essential to surviving on their own.

We start laying the foundation for that independence during our kid's first few years of school. It's during this time, when our kids are away from us for a few hours a day, that they slowly begin to learn how to take care of themselves—a skill that they'll have to draw on time and time again as they travel through life. Kids have to learn to keep track of all their stuff while they're off on their own—things like coats and hats and gloves and backpacks that have a way of disappearing if they're not paying attention. Learning to be respectful to everyone around them, even the kids they don't get along with, is another skill kids begin to learn as they navigate the school scene. These are life skills that transcend every grade and every age.

When you think about it, we're actually teaching our kids to learn to take care of themselves from the minute we bring our squishy little nuggets home from the hospital. That never stops. We put the squeaky toy just out of their reach to encourage them to start commando crawling; we put piles of Cheerios on their highchair tray to encourage them to feed themselves; and we talk to them incessantly, helping them build a vocabulary so that, ultimately, they can learn to communicate on their own.

You remember yourself at five or eight, right? Well I do, and if you're anything like me, you remember how heavily you relied on your mom and dad for **everything**. They were our money managers and cooking teachers. They were our shoe-tiers and chauffeurs. They were our caregivers and babysitters and playmates. They were our protectors. Now remember when you first started doing big things on your own? Like when you were twelve and got to stay home alone for the first time without a babysitter? Or when you got to use the stove for the first time? Or when you *became* the babysitter? Those milestones were big. Huge. And on some level, either consciously or unconsciously, we were grateful for our parents' vote of confidence.

So that's what we have to do as our kids make this move into the school system; we need to give them the independence that they're craving. Though it's their teacher who sets the bar for performing little day-to-day routines and tasks at school, like doing and passing in homework and collaborating with the other kids around them and remembering to be inclusive and kind to everyone, it's our job to reinforce all of those independent skills when our kids are back on our turf.

The point of all this is, the older our kids get, the more latitude we need to give them so they can start to handle things on their own. We need to encourage our kids to do things like manage their time and their friendships and their behavior and their stuff without our constant input or help. Because empowering our kids to think and do and speak for themselves is exactly how we raise healthy, independent kids who can thrive when they're out on their own in the big, wide world.

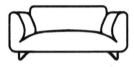

From the Couch of
Debra Fox Gansenberg MSW, LICSW

Though it may be easier to do a job yourself, the cost-benefit of having children do chores is important to consider: if you do those jobs yourself, you lose out in opportunities for teaching life lessons and skill building. Kids need opportunities to witness for themselves that they are capable, self-sufficient, and good at something they didn't think they could do.

Tip: Gen Zers are often known as the generation who have trouble with the simple things like eye contact, hand shaking, manners, and taking care of the simple stuff. Creating opportunities to teach these skills in the home is imperative for your children in order to behave the way we hope they would without us around. Create space and time for your kids to develop these life skills and try them out. Practice makes close to perfect.

Tip: Self-esteem is the single most important tool that any happy, healthy, and successful person must have! But it's not something you're born with. People you interact with, places that make you feel good, and skills you learn all build self-esteem. Be that person, in that place, doing those things and teaching those skills to help your child be self-assured. Self-esteem and confidence are more apt to grow when you attempt something and learn you can do it and possibly do it well.

Tip: Skill building for younger kids is a chance to work on fine and gross motor skills when pushing, stacking, or even wiping something. Also learning that going through a process that has a beginning, a middle, and an end may take a bit of time. Experiencing an eventual outcome will help teach delayed gratification. Gen Zers are used to immediate results due to the world they're growing up in where everything is a push of a button or swipe of a card away. Accomplishing something takes effort, motivation, and actual energy. Gen Zers find it hard to put it all together and navigate through to the end. Working through a chore is a great way to teach these skills.

Tip: Successful adults are people who can work well with others, take direction well, and have good self-discipline. Give your kids opportunities to work as a team, follow the directions, and meet expectations each week with a Saturday or Sunday chore day activity. Provide a model and join them. They often don't know how to do the simple things, so work as a family and rake the leaves in the yard. Offer an opportunity to enjoy the process and provide support, encouragement, and praise throughout the activity. Kids will gain a sense of accomplishment and pride, which is a necessary feeling to experience in order to navigate life.

Natural consequences tend to be the most impactful because they do not involve anyone trying to manipulate the outcome, it just happens. Providing the appropriate reminder or expectation is fine, but know when to draw the line so your child learns that he/she is responsible for the outcome.

Tip: Knowing when or where to draw the line when parenting is not an exact science; however, figuring it out along the way will definitely have a positive impact on discipling your children. Deciding when your job stops and your child's job starts doesn't have to be that difficult. Once you give your child clear, concise expectations, you need to step back and let them give it a try. See if there is traction between the message sent, the message received, and the actual action and output. If Sara doesn't remember to put her gym clothes into her backpack even after you provided a gentle reminder, she will mostly likely earn a natural consequence for this. You need to step back and let it happen.

Tip: Is it hard for you to watch your child fail or be disappointed? That is your issue not your child's. Part of growing up is feeling the successes and the failures. If Tommy forgets to bring his mittens to school and it is cold outside during recess, he might not be able to play football because his hands are too cold. Tommy might experience disappointment, but the chances of him forgetting his mittens the next time will be less likely, because he has gone through the process himself without you tampering. Remember, if you slide his mittens into his bag, he will learn that is part of the solution—so why bother when Mom's gonna do it.

Our process of family takes on different purposes. If parenting has been done successfully, there is the hope that children will want to spread their wings and fly. Parents need to step aside and create the space for this to happen.

Tip: Believe it or not, our goal as parents is to create a nest, fill it with chicks, grow the chicks and their wings, and watch them fly away, always to return to the nest when in need of rest. For some this is hard to even fathom; however, if we want to have children and see them ultimately succeed in all aspects of life, we need to help them grow wings in order to use them. Parents, we are living our lives as adults and it is our children's turn to do the same someday. If we do not create space for this to happen, we will have children who fail to launch. As a result, there will be a sense of dependency on us as parents that will lead to an unhealthy future for our kids.

Tip: The process of sending children into flight is actually greatly impacted by those sending them into flight. As an adult that was once nurtured in a family of origin, take some time to acknowledge how your journey went. Was it hard to flap your wings and head into flight? Was anyone holding you back or pushing you out prematurely? Do you return to your childhood nest as an adult and rejuvenate and recall pleasant times? If these questions poke at some issues that feel unresolved or complicated, seek a mental health professional to process these things and arrange them in a better place for you so that you can successfully launch your own chicks.

Tip: When you look back at your own family of origin, what were the roles like in the family? We often replicate the roles we witness as a child in our own adult life. The other scenario is doing the totally opposite to what we witnessed and experienced as a child. Nonetheless, we take our own experiences into the development of our new ones. Did you have a stay-at-home parent that was the full-time taxi, chef, and housekeeper? Was one parent always at work? As we discuss in this book, kids are watching us and learning, which all eventually impacts their future. Take some time to discuss with your parenting partner what the roles are in the family and understand how they might contribute to the outcome and process in the family of origin you are both developing.

Survival Tip 9:

Quit Comparing Yourself and Your Kids to Everyone Else

School is an amazing place, but all the comparing that comes along with it can be toxic, so watch out!

It's human nature to compare ourselves to the people around us. It just is. And there isn't one of us out there who doesn't do it on at least some level. Whether we're ranking ourselves for how tall or short we are or scrutinizing our marriage against our best friend's relationship, we're all prone to comparing ourselves to other people. It's just what we do. Unfortunately, that tendency to compare ourselves to the people around us only magnifies when we send our kids off to school.

Once we enter the world of The School System, we open ourselves, and our kids, to a whole new world of people and things that lend themselves to being compared against—like other moms and other dads and other kids. And that can be super-dangerous when we're parenting differently than the other parents out there or when our kids are learning or progressing at a different speed than the kids around them.

If you want to experience the joy of watching your child develop in school, while also helping them grow up healthy and comfortable in their own skin, avoid the trap of comparing your kid to other kids—or yourself to other parents. Instead, embrace sending your kids off to school and exposing them (and yourself) to all of the other beautiful influences that are around you, because that's where the magic happens. Just brace yourself hard against comparing how your kid learns versus the kids around them and know, going into the school experience, that the learning curve is super wide and everyone falls in a very different place along that curve.

Take it from a mom who's already sent two kids out into the big world: the best thing you can do for yourself and your child is to celebrate *their* accomplishments and *their* milestones and *their* pace. Because when you focus the lens onto what everyone around them is doing, that causes stress and anxiety in your kids and turns the learning process into something negative instead of the positive experience that it's supposed to be.

> 📖 **Parents are a child's first teacher, but it's not just up to us. Home, school, and community leaders educate our children. There is not just one part of the child that we need to grow; it is the whole child: academic, social, emotional, and behavioral.**

Kindergarten is the Foundation

Look, it's unlikely that your son will graduate from his kindergarten class knowing quantum field theory. Although if he does, then you might want to consider sending him directly to second grade. Or maybe grad school. But it *is* realistic to expect that most kids will leave kindergarten way more prepared for life than they were when they went in. That's because, when you really break it down, the skills that our kids learn—that we learned—in that first real year of school are among the most essential skills we all need as we move through life.

Think about it—by the time most kids graduate to first grade, they will have learned the alphabet, how to write words and simple sentences, how to count and share, how to name shapes and sort and classify objects, how to tell time, name the seasons, and, most importantly, how to work collaboratively with the people around them—and all in roughly 180 days, which is some pretty epic learning as far as I'm concerned. Some won't quite get to all of that, but others will go beyond their kindergarten curriculum. And that's okay.

Granted, some kids will arrive on their first day of kindergarten already knowing a lot of this stuff, or at least knowing some, but the majority of these skills will be learned and honed during the ten months they spend in that first year of school. It's these fundamental life skills that lay the foundation for everything that comes after. Like, everything. And that's a good thing, a great thing actually. All of these little daily nuances they're learning in the classroom—like manners and sharing and respect and not to pee on the circle time rug—will eventually trickle into their lives at home. And that makes our job a lot easier, because they're being reinforced by someone other than us.

Ask anyone who's spent any real time around young kids how quickly kids sponge up all the information around them and they'll tell you it's mind-blowing. While no two kids do it at the same speed, they are all learning an incredible amount of material and skills. I've watched it all first-hand. For years, when my own kids were in elementary school, I worked as an aide in kindergarten through third grade. The transformation I saw in those kids over the course of just those first few years in school was astounding. That's because so many of them enter kindergarten incapable of something as simple (for grown-ups at least) as sitting quietly at a table or transitioning from arts and crafts to music. But by June, most of them have evolved to a place where they can transition successfully between activities, work collaboratively with their teachers and their peers, and think creatively. This is exactly why kindergarten and those early years in school are such critical years for our kids—because they're learning the basic skills they need to adjust to being out in the real world.

I'm talking about the very things that Robert Fulghum talks about in his *New York Times* bestseller from the '80s, *All I Really Need to Know I Learned in Kindergarten*. When you get right down to it, Fulghum was a real visionary. He believed that "wisdom was not at the top of the graduate school mountain, but there in the sand pile at Sunday School." He says "everything you need to know is in there somewhere."[11] And I for one think he's absolutely right.

Check out his list below of some of the skills he learned while he was in kindergarten. Then apply each one to your daily life, whether it's your home life, your life as a parent, or your professional life, and see for yourself how each and every one of them translates to your everyday life.

- Share everything.
- Play fair.
- Don't hit people.
- Clean up your own mess.
- Don't take things that aren't yours.
- Say you're sorry when you hurt somebody.[12]

If you don't believe Mr. Fulghum, the folks at the Media Lab at the Massachusetts Institute of Technology (MIT) feel the same way. They think we should make the rest of school (like all the grade levels)—and life—more like kindergarten. According to a 2009 article in edutopia.org, the MIT guys see it this way: "As kindergartners playfully create stories, castles, and paintings with one another, they develop and refine their abilities to think creatively and work collaboratively, precisely the abilities most needed to achieve success and satisfaction in the 21st century."[13]

To be honest, some of the adults I know have forgotten that it's the basic people skills we learned when we were young that are the very foundation on which our adult lives and interactions are built.

That's why it's so important that you keep cool if everything doesn't click for your kids right away when they start school. Believe me, most skills take time to develop. Your child may be really great at smearing paint on tag board but struggle when it comes to listening during circle time. You, as the parent, need to avoid falling into the trap of measuring your kid up against all the other kids in class. You know, the ones in the other guided reading groups reading higher-level books or your daughter's friend who did more sit-ups during the Presidential Physical Fitness Test or your son's buddy whose artwork was picked to hang in the school lobby. Everything comes out in the wash. Kids find their own groove and settle into their stride at their own pace. Which is *exactly* what they're supposed to do. It's what we *all* have to learn to do. We need to chill a little and let our kids grow up at their pace. Because the sooner we learn this the better off we'll be.

> 📖 **Try to understand your child as an individual. Comparing kids to others can cause unnecessary worry and stress. While your child is growing and learning, consider the sequence as well as the rate of their development. Take some time to learn the difference so that you can meet the needs of *your* child.**

Kids find their own groove and settle into their stride at their own pace.

During that first experience with school, our kids have enough pressure on them just learning to separate from us every day, trying to fit into a different routine, and being introduced to so many new people and experiences. The very *last* thing they need is for us to be stacking them up against the kids around them and judging how they're adjusting. I'll give you one guess what that creates . . . Yup, it creates stress. And it builds tension and anxiety in us as well as in them.

When we're stressed, no matter how hard we try to hide it, our kids sense it. They have the uncanny ability to see right through us most of the time, especially when what we're trying to conceal concerns them. It's a lot like how our pets can sense when there's fear or sadness or illness. Kids are almost exactly the same, except for the shedding.

Once we cross over into that world of using other kids as benchmarks, we stop appreciating what our own kids have to offer. Consider this a warning, because once you start openly comparing your kids to the ones around them, that's exactly when they'll start doing the same. There are few things that can be more damaging to a growing child than constantly measuring themselves against other people. It's exhausting, it's pointless, and it can create a seriously insecure kid.

Remember, in school, just like in life, there's always going to be someone better, stronger, smarter, and faster than us—and our kids. Accepting this early on as parents will get rid of more frustration than you can imagine. Letting go of expectations frees everyone from getting caught in that trying-to-measure-up trap. In these first years of school, guide your children free of this trap, because the measuring up game only becomes bigger as your children advance from grade school to middle school and beyond. If you help them stay free from it now, it will be much easier to avoid as they grow.

Because once our kids move on to middle school and then high school, everyone becomes much more aware of who the "smart kids" are and who the "jocks" are, and competition really starts to heat up for a lot of our kids. This can cause some major insecurities down the line if our kids don't learn how to keep everyone's strengths and weaknesses in check—especially their own.

Once you accept that every kid is different and they all operate on their own unique developmental clock, you're ahead of the game. Tampering with your kid's clock too much by putting unrealistic pressure or expectations on them will be disastrous, but encouraging them to be true to themselves will show them that you've got their back and you support their decisions. When our kids feel supported, the sky is usually the limit.

> **Once you accept that every kid is different and they all operate on their own unique developmental clock, you're ahead of the game.**

You see, **there's a fine line between encouragement and pressure**. It's our job as parents to stay on the right side of that line. Because once you start telling your kids which sport to play or what instrument to choose or what language to study or which girls or boys they should be friends with, then you've taken away their ability to figure things out for themselves. Instead, you're persuading them to do what's good for you. They're not doing what *they* really want anymore. Instead of learning to listen to their inner voice and discover what they love, they are learning to please a parent. And that's not good.

> 🛋 **We want to encourage our children to create excitement, motivation, and desire to do well. However, there is a fine line between encouragement and pressure. Finding a good balance can be hard to do. Take time to figure out the difference, because their impact creates different outcomes.**

This All Applies to Parents Too

The other thing we need to avoid that's just as important as not measuring our kids against other kids, is not measuring *ourselves* against other parents. Because believe me, you'll want to. A lot. Especially once your kids get to school and you're exposed to all types of parents. Resist that urge, because it will make you second-guess every decision you make. Not to mention that comparing yourself to other parents will never make you a better parent. It won't help your sanity either!

It's hard, I know, because when you start interacting with other parents and kids on a day-to-day basis the temptation is high to measure yourself and your own parenting style against all the other parents you meet. You learn just how many different types of parents and styles of parenting there are out there, which inevitably leads us to question how we parent our own kids. You'll catch yourself trying to adapt all the approaches other parents use, expecting that you'll have the same results. And while some will work, others will be epic fails.

Once we start comparing ourselves to the parents around us, we start to question whether we're being strict enough or loose enough with our kids, and that can lead to making bad parenting decisions based only on how something worked for someone else. And that seems kinda dumb, doesn't it? This is exactly why you need to resist the urge to follow along. Not everything works for everyone. Each kid and parent and family is decidedly different.

Just remember, as you start this long and beautiful and sometimes challenging journey, that the learning curve for us as parents is almost as broad as it is for our kids. **There's no perfect path**. And the greatest thing we can do for our kids is to celebrate them for who they are as unique and beautiful little people and support them as they try to find their way. And that means giving them the slack they need to explore everything around them. It means giving them the latitude to fall and to fail and to choose, on their own, what appeals to them. Can you guide them? Absolutely. Should you drive the bus for them? Absolutely not. But here are a few ways you can help:

- Ask your kids what *they're* interested in and help them find opportunities to explore those things through groups, clubs, activities, or lessons.
- Reassure them that it's normal to fail at first but that screwing up is just part of how we all get better.
- If your kids aren't sure what they're interested in, offer to expose them to some of the things you love to see if any of those things light their fire.
- Consider your word choice when you're supporting your kid's choices and always lead with positive reinforcement and constructive feedback.
- Encourage your kids to go outside their comfort zone even if they're afraid of failing.
- When your kids try something new, always lead with positive

feedback like, "I love how you didn't stop until you got to the end of the race even though you hit some hurdles on the course."

- Focus on the times they succeed rather than the times they fail.
- Let them take the initiative as they discover what they like and what they don't like.
- Remind your kids to see a commitment through to the end, like a class or a sport or an activity, because sometimes we don't fall in love with things right away. Sometimes it takes times to develop a passion.

You've got a long way to go as you watch your kids grow and mature and work their way through the next twelve-plus years of school. I've watched my own girls stumble and fall and cry tears of joy and pain as they both tried to find their way, so I know how hard it can be as a parent to stay put on the sidelines and watch them play the game. It can be gut-wrenching. You have to though. Empowering them from the time they're young to make their own decisions and handle the consequences of their actions is one of the greatest gifts we can give our kids.

> **Empowering kids from the time they're young to make their own decisions and handle the consequences of their actions is one of the greatest gifts we can give our kids.**

Stoking our kid's academic career starts as soon as we send them off to school. Our kids don't suddenly become geniuses. So don't freak out if your third-grader doesn't come home with all As or check-pluses or whatever your school dishes out. We need to keep reminding ourselves that he's learning so much more than what is printed on a report card. There are a lot of moving parts that come along with school and not all of them can be quantified. In fact, most of them can't. Remember, every one of our kids is different, just like every parent is different. We have our own style and our own unique strengths and that's exactly how it's supposed to be. Just encourage your kids to try on lots of hats and see which ones fit best for them. They'll thank you for it later on, I promise.

From the Couch of
Debra Fox Gansenberg MSW, LICSW

Parents are a child's first teacher, but it's not just up to us. Home, school, and community leaders educate our children. There is not just one part of the child that we need to grow; it is the whole child: academic, social, emotional, and behavioral.

Tip: When watching your child grow and develop there are four main areas that you want to consider:

During the school year, we most often concern ourselves with our child's school experience; this is called their academic part. When we think of their academic part, we need to consider more than just the outcome of a grade. You want to pay attention to where they are in their development of skills, the type of learner they are, and areas of interest they have and like to learn about. Is there a subject that is harder than another due to concepts or teacher style? Take inventory throughout the year to better understand your child's academic strength and weaknesses in order to use this knowledge as they prepare for the following year.

Then there is their social part to be aware of, which includes whether or not they are finding success in connecting with their peer group in various situations. Are they extroverted or more introverted, do they play with others or spend more time alone? At school they might wear a different hat than at home; it can be fun to see how they develop in different settings.

The emotional part needs a lot of attention. What is their disposition at school? Are they smiling with their chin up or hunting for ants? Are they feeling confident and self-assured? When there is sharing time, do they participate and seem to be in a happy place or is there sadness or anger that is more prominent? A child's emotional health will impact all areas of development, so gain awareness of how they might be feeling.

Finally, there is their behavioral part that needs to be attended to. A child often will communicate how they are doing through their behavior, verbally or non-verbally. Are they able to resolve conflict and participate in problem solving, or do they get aggressive or withdraw? Can they sit still in their seat and attend to their work? Are they respecting others' personal space? Spend time observing in order to better understand what your child's needs might be. Their entire profile needs to be considered when educating the whole child. If you have concerns about any or all of these areas, ask questions, observe, and gather information from those involved in your child's life.

Tip: Working with families in homes and in schools gives a perspective of how a village can work together to raise our children. Don't be afraid to ask questions and get curious about where your child is going to school. They spend six hours of each day in their classroom, their second home. Sometimes their teachers and peers spend more time with them than we do in a day. If there are concerns about the classroom environment, policies, and rules, gain clarity so you can assist your child to find success. Consider all the aspects of your child's development. If you have any concerns, inquire as your child's teachers are your eyes during the school day. Ask them what they observe and experience. Knowledge is power and can help assess if the environment is the appropriate place for your child's learning. Make sure their school is the correct placement for their needs.

Try to understand your child as an individual. Comparing kids to others can cause unnecessary worry and stress. While your child is growing and learning, consider the sequence as well as the rate of their development. Take some time to learn the difference so that you can meet the needs of your child.

Tip: Do you remember learning how to read as a kid? Some learned to read in preschool while others learned to read in kindergarten, and others in first or second grade. Guess what—in the long run it really doesn't matter when you learned, as long as the skill was eventually mastered. When you find yourself in a conversation of preschool comparison, give yourself permission to step back and remove yourself from it. The secret about reading, along with most skills, is that kids progress as they develop. There may be a "normal" sequence to learning that comes with benchmarks in each grade level, but this is primarily used to help gauge how your child is making progress. The rate at which your child learns is actually the speed that they learn, and that is also monitored. There are often cases where the child's output, or lack thereof, is teaching us that there might be a learning difference or challenge that could need attention; this is why comparing kids could create additional stress or concern. There are plenty of resources and support services to help every kind of student.

We want to encourage our children to create excitement, motivation, and desire to do well. However, there is a fine line between encouragement and pressure. Finding a good balance can be hard to do. Take time to figure out the difference, because their impacts create different outcomes.

Tip: Can you recall a time that you were encouraged; how did it make you feel? Another definition of "encourage" is "to inspire, invigorate, motivate, or support." All of these synonyms are *feel good* words. When you give encouragement to your child with kind words or thoughtful actions, the chance of your child finding energy, enthusiasm, and desire to do something is much greater. When you are encouraged, it can warm your heart and fill you with excitement.

Tip: We want what is best for our children, and at times our intention is to support them but we use a different kind of energy when we are trying to help. Our words and actions can turn into pressure. How many of us nag, pester, or even demand things of our children? The application of our encouragement goes one step further and turns into a *hard sell*. We need to be careful our requests are not filled with an energy that actually will dissuade or repress our kids during a time when they need to accomplish or attempt to do something. One might feel heavy in the chest and anxious in the belly when feeling pressure. Choose your words carefully and be mindful of your actions. You want to help your kids, not hurt them.

Tip: Check in with yourself, Mom and Dad. We often repeat what was done to us as kids. Were you encouraged as a child? Were your family members jumping up and down when you were up at bat or in a spelling bee? Did their excitement create the energy to try your best and not worry about whether or not you struck out or hit a home run? Did you feel proud of yourself and want to do the best you can? If you are nodding your head, yes, then you experienced encouragement.

How about the time you spelled the word wrong and lost the spelling bee; did someone get upset with you because you knew how to spell the word you got wrong? Did you hang your head in embarrassment and worry because you knew your parents were going to be disappointed? Did you think: *I will never do this again because my parents thought I was going to win, I can't bear the feeling of failure?* Pressure is what you experienced, and it is something hard to forget. Take some time to help those parts of you that tend to pressure your kids and evolve them into a better outcome. Recall what pressure did to you and try and slow it down and back yourself up before you do to your child what was done to you.

Survival Tip 10:

Make School Drop-offs Quick, Like Ripping off a Band-Aid

Because when you linger, your kid lingers, and then nobody goes anywhere.

For Survival Tip 8, we talked about letting go so our kids can learn a little independence and how school can play a big role in that learning process. That means getting used to an entirely new routine—a routine that, for many, involves spending almost as much time away from each other as you spend together. Adapting to that separation is never easy for us or for our kids.

Walking into a brand-new environment, filled with brand-new everything, usually produces two distinctly different reactions from our kids. Some of them will embrace the change and drop your hand and go, while others will grab onto your pant leg like a pit bull and hang on for dear life. It's a crapshoot, really, in terms of which kids will react which way.

> 🛋 **We have more influence on our children than we realize. It is important to understand our facial expressions are a reflection that they see all the time. Be mindful that when you look sad as they are hopping out of the car at drop-off, that can influence them to feel sad too.**

Just Turn and Go

That's why the best thing we can do for our daughter or son who just turns and runs happily into the classroom is to turn away ourselves and leave. Just leave, so they can learn to find their own way. Let them cast their net and haul in their own catch.

When your son is hugging your leg like it's a tree in a hurricane, pry him off and encourage him to find a friend or join a team or explore a hobby. If he struggles at first, you also need to turn away and leave. This is the critical point when our kids have to start learning to rely on themselves and on people other than Mom and Dad. And we have to find a way to be okay with that.

See, even though we're so used to being joined at the hip that we'd just as soon pick him up and bring him home and try again another year, we can't. We have to start fraying the umbilical cord. We don't have to cut it altogether, but we do have to gear ourselves up to cut it eventually to help our kids become more independent.

Giving our kids the right amount of space to develop a sense of independence and to learn to think for themselves is usually much easier said than done. But it *is* possible, and it's very, very necessary. Knowing how to separate is a big step toward making that happen. Whether it's the first day of kindergarten or the first day of seventh grade, you need to know how to say good-bye. Separation anxiety isn't just reserved for toddlers and young kids; it can just as easily impact tweens and even teenagers.

> **Whether it's the first day of kindergarten or the first day of seventh grade, you need to know how to say good-bye.**

The question then becomes: Do you just pat your daughter on the tush and push her in the direction of the classroom door, or do you prolong the painful good-bye until she's ready to leave you?

The answer: You leave! And fast! In fact, run! Because **if you don't leave, she won't leave** and if she won't leave, then you've got yourself a problem with potentially ugly consequences. You can imagine what that must look like. It's not pretty. Believe me, I've seen it up close. It involves crying and flailing and kicking and screaming—and that's just the parents.

After years and years in elementary school classrooms and front offices, you can bet I've seen some pretty dicey drop-off disasters—everything ranging from crying moms and shrieking kids to full-on floor slamming meltdowns and door-grabbing tantrums. I've seen both the ugly and the nasty, and not just in the lower grades. I've watched kids bolt across the playground after their parents' car; I've seen them lock themselves in bathroom stalls; I've seen kids literally hog-tie themselves to their parent's leg. Name it and I've probably seen it.

Take the fourth-grade girl in the classroom down the hall from mine who refused to get out of the car every morning. Monday through Friday she held onto seat belts or car doors as a way of avoiding going to school. Her parents were super passive about it, letting her dictate how long the tantrums would last. They let her get away with making her own rules and did very little to discourage the behavior. There was kicking and yelling and thrashing. Most days there was a full-body collapse that forced her dad to have to carry her, limp, into the building so he could get to work. Ironically, as soon as she got into the classroom, she was fine. This is a perfect example of why it's so important for us to lay down real expectations and then hold our kids accountable for their behavior.

Let's put it in different terms. You've tried taking a Band-Aid off slowly, right? Well, it kills and usually leaves a blotchy red mark. But rip it off quickly and it only stings for a second and you're over it. Well, separating from our kids works basically the same way. The longer we drag out our good-byes, the more painful it is to let go and the bigger the emotional mark is left. For everyone—including the staff in the main office watching the show.

I know it hurts. Letting go of our kids, even just a little bit, rips at your heart. Sometimes I'm honestly not sure who it hurts more, us or them? We'll call it a tie, for argument's sake.

Maybe you've been lucky up to this point and you haven't had any separation issues with your kids. And if you haven't had any dicey moments yet, consider yourself blessed, because separation anxiety can be stressful for everybody.

The reality is, though, that even though you may have dodged the bullet up to now, it's probably unlikely that you'll dodge it altogether. As those of us with kids know, parenthood is not a straight line, and things don't always happen exactly the way they tell us they will in Lamaze class. Just because certain milestones or behaviors appear more often at specific ages doesn't mean they're relegated to those ages. You'll learn pretty quickly (if you haven't already) that anything can happen at any time. **That's why we have to be as nimble as we can, because the ground is constantly shifting under our feet**.

That fear of being separated can manifest any time in many different ways, ranging from being clingy and suction-cupped to your side to being scared of strangers and throwing tantrums, and it can be a tricky phase to handle. Although this stage is usually temporary and more common in young kids ages eight to fourteen months old, it's also seen in teenagers. Managing that kind of anxiety in teens can be equally as tough, because separation anxiety in older kids can look like everything from an upset stomach or headaches to insomnia or panic attacks. It really is best to help kids learn, starting at an early age, that separating from Mom and Dad can be tough, but it is manageable.

When it comes to separation issues, you have to understand what the child is going through. Even though *we* know we'll always come back, our kids don't. No amount of reasoning with them in the heat of their separation anxiety free fall can convince them that you will. That's because the wiring in their kid brains just isn't developed enough yet to grasp that we mean what we say. They're too overcome by big, scary nerves that take the logic out of everything.

I can't say that I blame kids for freaking out, because, when you think about it, we've been their main go-to people pretty much since they were born. We fed them and cuddled them and clothed and nurtured them, and now we're up and leaving them for *X* number of hours each day with people they don't really know. Honestly, I'd be bummed out too. It makes perfect sense that they're funky about separating from us. We've been their security blanket all this time, and we all know how tough it is to give up our woobie. It's tough. But as you'll notice when you look around you, it can be done, otherwise we'd be seeing an awful lot of high school kids dragging ratty looking blankies with them all over town.

    💬 **Separation anxiety is a common developmental stage for most older infants, toddlers, and school-age children.**

The experience may not be pleasant, but it is typically short-lived. Parents can make good-byes easier by making sure their own emotions don't get in the way.

The good news is that separation anxiety is usually a pretty short-lived phenomenon. In other words, *this is a phase.* How long we're stuck in the thick of it is pretty heavily dependent on us and how we handle ourselves as parents.

I guess you could say this is one of the first times that we really have to parent-up. Remember the blinking game we all played when we were kids? The one where we forced our eyes to stay open and resisted the urge to blink first no matter what. Tears would be streaming down our cheeks and our eyes would be burning, but we refused to give in. We got props for being tough. When we won, we earned respect.

Well, dealing with a sad, crying kid at drop-off is the grown-up version of that game, only now we're playing against our kids. **And we can't blink first!** You get me? If we blink first, we lose all our street cred. If we're the first to cave, then our kids learn, in that one instant, that they can beat us. Then it's game over.

If we're the first to cave, then our kids learn, in that one instant, that they can beat us.

So our only job now is to convince our teary-eyed son that we're coming back at the end of the school day. How do we do that? Simple. We reassure him, every day, that we're going to be waiting outside after school exactly where we're supposed to be. And then be there. It's that simple. Day in and day out we're going to be in that spot, waiting. Day after day, our son is going to see that we're coming back, just like we told him we would that morning at drop-off. We call this positive reinforcement. Believe me, it works.

What about the Tears?

Here's one pitfall to watch out for: our kids learn very early in life how to leverage our love for them to their advantage. They know exactly when squirting out a few tears will get them what they want, and they're not afraid to use this power against us every chance they get. That's why you'll often see them coincidentally start to well up *just* as you're turning to leave them at school. As long as you stay strong and committed to the drop-off, both you and your kids will be fine.

There are certain critical crossroads we reach as parents, and the direction we choose to go dictates how bumpy the road is from that point on. Like the intersection we reach when we put our newborn down to sleep in their own room for the first time, and the second we walk out the door they start crying. Do we run back in and scoop them up, or do we let them learn, a little bit at a time, how to soothe themselves? In that moment, we're at one of these junctures when we have to decide which direction to go and our journey will change drastically depending on which direction we choose. Either we keep running back in every time our baby cries and reinforce that we'll always come when they cry, or we resist the impulse and hold our ground. We wait five minutes and then go to them. Then we wait ten minutes. Then twenty after that. Then, usually in a few days, we have a baby who can self-soothe herself to sleep. BOOM!

This is the cry-it-out method Dr. Benjamin Spock recommended back in the mid-forties. His philosophy was so simple—the sooner babies learned how to self-soothe, the better off they'd be—and the better off we'd be, too, in the long run. And wouldn't you know, for the most part, he was right, at least in my house. This approach holds true today and applies to so much more than just sleeping. After all, how do you think any of us learned how to swim or walk or talk? Someone was holding on to us in the beginning and, eventually, they let go. See my point?

Okay, back to drop-off anxiety. Why can some kids just trot off to school without even needing to say good-bye? Well, as it happens, some kids are just born a little more anxious than others. That's all. Some are born good swimmers, some have perfect pitch, some have night terrors. Some are outgoing while others are more conservative by nature. It's just the luck of the genetics draw. The thing is, though, as much as certain aspects of our kids' behavior is biological, a lot of it has to do with us and how we parent them. If we yell, chances are good they'll yell. If we hit, they'll hit. If we're obnoxious, our kids are most likely going to be obnoxious, and so on. If we make an effort to be calm and rational when we're with our kids, then the over-under is pretty high that that's what they'll pick up on after time.

Along with maintaining a good, positive attitude around our children, like we talked about in Survival Tip 1, there are plenty of other things that we can do to help our anxious kids to be a little more relaxed. These things are easy and fun for both us and them.

Remind Our Kids We're Still Thinking of Them, Even When We're Not Together

I was a big note-writer when my kids were in school. Still am, actually. I got it from my mom who was notorious for sending me sweet little just-thinking-of-you notes in my lunch when I was a kid. I loved her little messages because they were a way of connecting with her while I was at school and we were apart. They were also the perfect little reminder that she was thinking of me, too, during the day. To this day, I still write my girls notes on special occasions, like when they've got a big test or a track meet. Even though they're reluctant to admit it sometimes, they've both fessed up that they still love it. Another idea is to establish a special morning/afternoon ritual that you can do together every day, like a crazy handshake before your son leaves for school and again when he climbs back in the car at the end of the day.

> 🛋 **Transitions can be hard for everyone, whether it's getting up in the morning and going to school or getting dropped off to the sitter. Take time to observe how your child manages transitions to see what they might need to transition with more ease.**

To help with that home-to-school transition, maybe build a little more time into the morning routine so that everyone stays relaxed and happy. If getting out of the house in the morning is stressful, that stress is going to bleed into the drop-off and into the rest of everyone's day. If you often arrive to school a little too early, before most of the other kids are there, wait a few extra minutes to leave the house to ensure your kid has someone to wait with and doesn't need you for support. Starting out the school day with a friend can make good-byes easier.

It's things like hiding notes in their lunches, making good-byes short and sweet, and anticipating a little extra funkiness on Monday mornings that help give us a competitive edge against separation anxiety. It's being mindful of these things that makes the transition to the school routine and other activities easier on us and on our kids.

Here's a free tip: **parenting is really all about the follow through**. It's about saying what we mean and meaning what we say—at least the majority of the time. The most successful parents are almost always the ones who consistently put their money where their mouth is and follow through with things like consequences or actions or promises. The truth is, it only takes a few times digging in our heels and holding the line for our kids to realize that we mean business. That's really all they need to know. Whether they're conscious of it or not (and most aren't), our kids take great comfort in having limits and boundaries. Our job as parents is to remember that it's our responsibility not only to set the boundaries, but to enforce them as well.

> **Whether they're conscious of it or not, our kids take great comfort in having limits and boundaries.**

Look, drop-off drama is real and it can be gut-wrenching and debilitating for everybody if it's not managed. But it's normal—I repeat, it's normal—and it usually doesn't last forever. But confidence doesn't happen overnight, it's learned a little at a time. Have faith that your kids can and will stand on their own two feet. Once our kids mature a little and cultivate their own coping mechanisms, recognizing that we'll always be there for the pickup, drama over being separated usually resolves itself—hence the lack of teddy bears in college dorms.

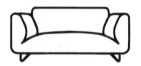

From the Couch of
Debra Fox Gansenberg MSW, LICSW

We have more influence on our children than we realize. It is important to understand our facial expressions are a reflection that they see all the time. Be mindful that when you look sad as they are hopping out of the car at drop-off, that can influence them to feel sad too.

   Tip: Have you ever heard the saying "Your eyes are the window into your soul"? What you put out to the universe through your eyes is sharing what you are feeling on the inside. Face-to-face communication increases the chances of understanding how the other person is feeling. Now factor in the understanding and interpretation of a young child seeing your facial expressions. If they see Mom tearing up on the first day of kindergarten they might think what they are about to do is not good or making you sad, so the child will be concerned. If you smile and your eyes are happy, then you are encouraging your child to feel the same way and they will proceed without concern.

Tip: Learning how to read facial expressions is an important skill for your child to learn. Kids who can read facial cues and social cues are more successful making friends and managing situations throughout their day. Help your child learn how to read others' facial expressions by modeling and practicing during playground time or a playdate. Ask your child to make facial expressions in the mirror and name the feeling they are trying to communicate. This is a great way to learn about what your child is trying to communicate.

Message: Your facial expressions are cues that can influence the mood of those around you. Help connect feeling words to facial expressions so that your children have a feelings vocabulary. If you want to have a wonderful day put on a happy face—it can impact your child's kind of day too!

Separation anxiety is a common developmental stage for most older infants, toddlers, and school-age children. The experience may not be pleasant, but it is typically short-lived. Parents can make good-byes easier by making sure their own emotions don't get in the way.

Tip: If you have an infant, toddler, or even elementary-school-aged student, separating can be quite difficult. However, sometimes their unwillingness to separate can be seen as a good sign that your child has made a healthy attachment to you. In this case, make the departure quick and simple so the suffering is not prolonged. The caregivers on the other side are there to reassure them with a hug and a smile.

Tip: Separation is hard because young children realize that there is only one of you and, when he/she can't see you, you've gone away. They don't understand when or if you'll be back; this is where the anxiety comes forward. That is why it is always recommended that you remind your child at any age that you will be returning, coming home, or picking them up again soon.

Tip: If your school-aged child is showing signs of distress when separating from you, their anxiety could be more intensive and their bodies might not be able to handle it well. It is important to get help for your child in the guidance department of their school to discuss if their separation anxiety is interrupting their daily process. There are systems that can be put in place to help ease your child's worries so they can enter the school successfully and manage when you leave.

Message: As parents, we have a direct impact on how successful our actual separation from our children goes. We need to work with our own anxious parts and get them to step back so that each departure is successful for everyone. Paint on a smile, remind them you will be back soon, and quickly walk away.

Transitions can be hard for everyone, whether it's getting up in the morning and going to school or getting dropped off to the sitter. Take time to observe how your child manages transitions to see what they might need to transition with more ease.

Tip: Our kid's days are constantly filled with transitions—from lunch to recess, gym to math, and school to swim team. It can be hard to follow directions, stay on task, and keep up with classmates, so giving them lessons along the way might help. Create lists or use timers to help kids remember what they need to do and pay attention to time. The more you can get them to practice, the greater success they will have keeping up in the classroom.

Tip: For young children, the transition away from home to a school, an activity, or a birthday party can be overwhelming to say the least. Send them with a transitional object, something that is small that can fit in their pocket that reminds them of you. This object will help them go from one place to the next while holding on to a little piece of you. A small picture, stick-it note, or worry stone are all great objects to put in their backpack and take a peek at when they are missing you. If your child shows signs of excessive crying, inability to let you go, or is inconsolable, enlisting help to assist in transitions might help.

Tip: Take a minute to look at how you, as an adult, manage transitions. Do you set alarms to remind you to be somewhere? Are you typically punctual or do you run late because you can get wrapped up in an activity and lose track of time? The apple doesn't fall far from the tree. Make sure you set examples of good time management, setting priorities, and leaving on time so that no one is rushing. You might be surprised how good habits can rub off.

Message: Our society is fast-paced and very busy. It is important to slow things down, take your time, and make sure you are giving everything you can to your child so that they can separate from you successfully.

Survival Tip 11:

Encourage Your Kids to Branch Out

Don't worry that they're getting more social . . . you'll always be their mom and dad

Now that our kids are in school and spending time with lots of new faces, like classmates and teachers and other parents, you might be feeling a little insecure, worrying that you're getting replaced by all these new people. It's totally normal to feel a little threatened by all the new people and influences in your kid's life because, well, they're new people and new influences and those can be scary, as much for us as for our kids. You're not being replaced though, I promise. And your kids need to expand their world, as much as we'd love to just bubble wrap them and keep them just for ourselves.

The simple truth is that, once our kids are old enough to develop meaningful friendships with other people, we need to encourage them to reach out to the world. This in no way means that they're forgetting us, even though it feels that way the older and more independent they get. You just have to remember who your daughter's first legitimate best friend was. *It was you.* And in many ways, you always will be. We all just need to come to terms with the idea that we're all going to be spending a lot more time apart. But that doesn't have to be a bad thing. In fact, when we encourage our kids to seek out and make new friends, it's a win-win for everyone, because we're helping our children hone the social and interpersonal skills they need to create their own little community. We're ensuring that they'll never be alone when we're not around. Plus, we're also regaining a little of our own independence and that can be a beeeeeeautiful thing!

As parents, we have to learn to digest the idea that we're not the only ones in our child's world anymore. The first time that really becomes obvious to us is when we see the new lineup of people that our kids are interacting with on a daily basis once they start school. Even if you're homeschooling your kids, this is the time they're likely to start meeting a lot of new people through homeschool groups or sports or clubs and extracurricular activities they get involved with. This is when they start recognizing that the world is much, much bigger than their yard or neighborhood or town. And even though it's intimidating, it's also very, very necessary that our kids learn to be comfortable branching out on their own.

We All Need to Find Our Tribe

Remember, in the same way friendship benefits us, our kids need different kinds of companionship and influences to stimulate their emotional, intellectual, and personal growth. Because without other outside influences, our kids have no real way of learning how to interact socially or how to be a good friend or how to be patient or nice or take turns or collaborate with the people around them. Even though they're not necessarily going to be best friends with everyone they meet, they still need to be exposed to all types of personalities to prepare them for what life is like in the real world when we're not there to plan and schedule and screen their playdates. Don't worry too much about being replaced though, because we'll always be on our kid's short list, no matter how many other people come into their life.

I guess I'm saying that one of the important things to keep in mind is that we're constantly interacting with new people at every stage of life, so the sooner we give our kids the skills and the bandwidth to branch out and build new relationships, the more equipped they'll be to handle their relationships as they move through elementary and middle school and ultimately to high school and college and the big, wide world.

📖 **Relationships are important for our children's mental, physical, and emotional health. The sooner we give our kids the skills to branch out and build new relationships, the more equipped they'll be to handle their relationships later in life.**

As our kids get older, they just need more stimulation and perspectives and viewpoints than they can get from us alone. Bob Livingstone, LCSW, offers a great list of why it's so important for kids to have friends:

- Creating friendships develops life skills that will increase your child's wisdom, confidence, and self-esteem.
- They'll learn that a good friend will have their best interests at heart and have their back. They'll also learn that someone who is not your friend will not have these qualities.
- Because friendship isn't always easy, it teaches kids how to deal with conflict and adversity.
- They'll have peers to share their concerns, dreams and fears with, which will make them feel less alone and isolated.
- When they become older, they'll have childhood memories to fall back on—remembering how joyful it was to hang out with friends.
- Kids playing together will learn to create interesting, collaborative activities.
- The opportunity to develop leadership skills increases as our kids play with other kids.
- The ability to make decisions is increased when children play with peers without micromanaging from adults.
- Free play with other children helps kids develop their imagination.
- Playing with lots of different kids allows our kids to see how other families operate, so they won't be shocked when faced with a family situation that's different from their own.[14]

Friendships without the Drama

Of course, the easiest and most obvious time for kids to make friends is when they're young because that's when they're surrounded by their first real crop of new faces and new opportunities, and younger kids aren't overly self-aware yet or preoccupied by things like social status and reputation. In other words, the playing field is pretty level.

It's in the first few years our kids are in school that there are no real party lines to worry about in terms of making friends. Boys are friends with girls just as comfortably as boys are friends with other boys and the same goes for girls. Future jocks are friends with future nerds and future tomboys play with future fashion designers.

Not to get too technical, but that's because gender and cliques are meaningless when our kids are just starting out. Cooties haven't gone mainstream and everyone's pretty androgynous. In other words, it's pretty much just a giant lovefest. Even more significant than that, *there's no drama*. So my advice to you is to enjoy the calm before the storm while you can. Because the drama storm *will* come. You remember the tornado in *The Wizard of Oz*, right?

In grammar school, your daughter's biggest social issue will most likely involve her crying over actual spilt milk. Other than that, friendship conflicts at that age are relatively harmless. *That's **my** eraser top! NO! It's **my** eraser top! That's **my** juice box! NO! It's **my** juice box!* (All those little square boxes look alike.) Honestly, that's about the worst of it.

This is the stage where giving our kids advice about friendship is pretty easy. When we're talking about new friends, all we have to say is, *You don't have to like everyone you meet. Because you won't. But you do have to be nice to everyone no matter what.* In the lower grades, it's usually that easy. Because in those early years, when our kids are still young, there isn't the social hierarchy and drama that you see in middle school and into high school.

> 🛋 **Learning how to make friends hasn't changed much since we were kids. You want to find ways to assist your child while being mindful that your process does not influence their experience in any way. Oftentimes we are experiencing our child's developmental process while also being reminded of our own.**

When they're young and making new friends, it is still pretty basic and straightforward. Here are some easy ways to help your younger kids bridge the gap:

- Every day after school, check in with your kids about who they're spending their time with during the day. Ask who they're playing with at recess or sitting with at lunch and find out if there's someone in particular they're getting close to.

- Encourage your children to reach out to a potential new friend to have a playdate or hang out after school.
- Encourage your kids to practice saying "Hi" to someone new by making good eye contact, smiling, and introducing themselves.
- Arrange a playdate at home where your child can feel comfortable on their own turf.
- Sign your child up for a sport or activity with a new friend so they can have an opportunity to get to know each other better.

Navigating Middle School Waters

The older our kids get, though, the more challenging it is to make and keep friendships. That's because, according to Eileen Kennedy-Moore, a clinical psychologist and author of *Smart Parenting for Smart Kids*, "children start to worry about friendship issues around age seven, when they hit an extremely judgmental phase of their cognitive development."[15] And once the lightbulb goes off and they become aware that there's a social hierarchy, there's no turning back. From the point, when our kids start putting other kids in categories like popular, geek, nerd, and jock, it's hard for them to ever think of the kids around them any other way, so reaching out and trying to make new friends becomes trickier because kids are way more focused on rejection and not fitting in than ever before.

Here are some ideas from The Inspired Treehouse to help your older kids navigate those often-muddy friendship waters:

1. **Read the room.** Encourage your kid to seek out others who look like they don't know a lot of people either. It's easier to engage with another new person who isn't familiar with the group than someone already enmeshed in a close crowd of friends.
2. **Gain attention.** The first thing you say to someone new should be warm, brief, and polite—just enough to get them to shift their attention to you. Encourage your child to practice using simple *interrupting words* such as: hello, excuse me, oh hey, or good morning. Model these words for your child and practice by pretending and role playing.
3. **Get in there.** Once you have someone's attention, ask for what you want. Show your child how to give the other person a concrete call to action with a yes/no question. This could be as simple as

"Can I sit with you?" or "Want to play basketball?" When there's a clear invitation to interact, most people will say "yes."

4. **Introduce yourself.** Once you're in there, either sitting at the table, playing the game, or working on the group project, let them know who you are. Demonstrate how your child could introduce himself, giving a simple detail or bit of information to show who he is. "Hi, I'm Ben. I'm in Miss Smith's class."

5. **Connect and stand out.** Once you've approached someone, gotten her attention, joined her group, and told her who you are, it's time to find some common ground. Give your child examples of questions she can ask to discover what she has in common with a new friend. This link can lead to further conversation and help her stand out from others in a positive way.[16]

The fact is, kids grow up. Sorry to be a spoiler, but it's just what happens. Even though most of us would love to freeze our little pocket-sized pumpkins exactly the way they are right now, we can't. Our smartest move as parents is to embrace the idea that *change is good*. Because change, she's a comin'. And she's comin' fast. That's why we need to trust in the fact that every stage with our kids will be more blissful than the last. (I'm laughing out loud now.)

Parenting is a free-for-all, I don't care what anyone says. No class or book or nugget of wisdom from our own parents can prepare us for what the real reality show is like. And once our kids leave the safety and security of the BabyBjörn for the real world, all bets are off.

The only thing I can tell you for sure is that the ground will always shift under our feet just as soon as we get our bearings. Once we get used to one stage, the next one comes and knocks us off balance. That's just parenthood. Fortunately for us, this growing up thing happens just gradually enough so we can manage to hang on. One of the biggest changes we have to accept once our kids reach school-age is that they're going to have a world full of new faces rotating in and out of their lives from this point on. The best thing we can do for them, even though we all know it's not easy, is to step aside and encourage them to reach out and make new connections. As hard as it is, it's our responsibility as parents.

These new relationships are critical to our children's social and emotional development, because they give our kids the opportunity to interact with all different kinds of people in all different types of situations. Even though we're only talking about elementary and middle school, that still represents a much bigger world than the one they've been used to up to now. And it just continues to expand the older they get.

> 📖 **New relationships are critical to our children's social and emotional development. Seeing a friendship through its different stages of growth is a worthwhile life experience. It gives our kids the opportunity to interact with different kinds of people in all different types of situations.**

People will constantly cycle in and out of our kid's lives at different points and for different reasons, and some will stay for the duration. Just try to remember that no matter how many people come and go in our kids' lives, we're always going to be the constant. Our job is to be the ones they can always count on regardless of who else is in the picture. But it's also our job to ensure that our kids have the skills they need to create their own network of people to bond and share their life with. Because we all need people in our life for everything from support and love to inspiration and security. So start helping your kids nurture and grow their relationships early, because the payoff is huge on the backside.

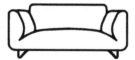

From the Couch of
Debra Fox Gansenberg MSW, LICSW

Relationships are important for our children's mental, physical, and emotional health. The sooner we give our kids the skills to branch out and build new relationships, the more equipped they'll be to handle their relationships later in life. The first experiences our children have to build relationships are with their parents, siblings, and relatives. Learning to feel love, cared for, and safe are all important aspects for their development. Healthy attachments are imperative for our children, and their family of origin is where it all begins. The family is the foundation for their personality, choices, and behavior.

Tip: What is a healthy attachment? It is the physical and emotional bond that develops between child and parents, often referred to as a family bond. These bonds set the stage for your child to begin developing their own social and emotional skills, which will influence a child's mental health and well being in the future. There are many easy ways to nurture your relationships with your children.

- Tell your child that you love them with verbal messages and physical affection.
- Spend time together playing, eating together at meal time, or a special nighttime routine.
- Establish your own special name for each other that is only used between family members.
- Set time aside in your day to check in with your child to learn how they are feeling and what they may need, showing care and concern for him/her.

Tip: Building relationships early in life can be done in very simple ways with family or friends. Simply create opportunities to share, take turns, and work together in a group to experience what it might be like to help someone and work as a team. In this environment, your child will learn to encourage, trust, and support one another, which are all the beginning foundations to any good relationship.

Tip: Another very important ingredient when teaching children how to have a healthy relationship is the concept of mutual respect. Teaching kids to use kind words and actions, as well as good listening ears, are all parts to showing how their relationship is two-sided and that your child should receive all which he gave in return.

Learning how to make friends hasn't changed much since we were kids. You want to find ways to assist your child while being mindful that your process does not influence their experience in any way. Oftentimes we are experiencing our child's developmental process while also being reminded of our own.

Do you remember how hard it was to find a friend out at recess to play with? Were you the last one picked to play basketball or were you the team captain picking all the teams? Our own journey of friendship seeking can really impact how we navigate this for our children. Did your mom want you to hang with the popular girls? Did Dad want you hang with the jocks? There are so many ways a child can be influenced when making friends, make sure you give them space to create and navigate their own process.

Tip: The most powerful tool in your child's kit when thinking about making a friend is the need for self-esteem and confidence. While parents can't make friends for them, they can help them practice until they feel more comfortable and confident to do it on their own. Practice salutations, how to get your buddy's attention. Create a conversation or dialogue that they can use when they have the opportunity to engage their classmate. Role model the possible scenario and practice until your child seems more self-assured and capable to give it a go.

Tip: The skill of making a friend hasn't changed too much, but there are new variables to consider. With constant contact, social media, and the good old house phone, our kids are supplied with many ways to actually reach out and connect. Begin by discussing which tool might work best for your child. Understanding if face-to-face conversation or texting back-and-forth would be best. It may be time to update your communication system and step back to entertain the new ways kids connect whether they call, text, tweet, or DM, they eventually make it happen.

Tip: Be supportive and careful not to influence your child in ways that might have happened to you as a kid. "Ben, are you sure you want to go to Tom's house; isn't he a troublemaker?" or "Jojo is kinda boring, isn't she? Are you sure you want to play with her at recess?" are not the kind of phrases we should use. Remember, let your child find the kids they are curious about, and let them navigate their own way. Rely on natural consequences to occur when or if they have made a poor selection for a playmate.

Friendships are important. It is not how many friends you have; it's about making a healthy connection with that special person that enriches your life, is supportive, and brings joy and happiness to your day. Encourage your children to keep at it until they feel what it is like to look down the hall and smile at that one classmate that they hope is their friend and receive a smile back.

New relationships are critical to our children's social and emotional development. Seeing a friendship through its different stages of growth is a worthwhile life experience. It gives our kids the opportunity to interact with different kinds of people in all different types of situations.
We experience all types of friendships in life. Some friendships last for years and evolve into a meaning relationship in our life, while others are more of a casual friend or acquaintance that, over time, might end. Teaching kids that there are different types of friendships will help as they travel through some of their first few experiences. Sharing some of your own stories might be a nice way to help.

Tip: The first step to building a solid friendship is your selection of the person you would like to embark on the endeavor with. How do you know if they are going to make a good friend? Teach your child the good ol' golden rule. Discuss the qualities that make up a good friend. Assist your child in recognizing their own special qualities and help them learn how to spot them in others. Follow up with a chat about what they expect from their good friend and what they think this friendship might look like.

Tip: Once you find a good person to befriend, it needs to be mutual by showing interest and commitment to get together—at recess to chat, after school to walk home, or a playdate over the weekend. This is the beginning stages which are commonly achieved by many young children. The next stage can be difficult without the involvement of a parent. This stage includes maintaining the friendship by finding things in common that you both enjoy, creating time to enjoy these activities together, and beginning to confide thoughts and feelings with each other. This is often referred to as "joined at the hip." As the friendship matures, there is trust and support that begins to shape with problem solving and lots of sharing, there is a lot of value in the emotional closeness as friends. This is typically where many kids arrive and tend to linger for years.

Tip: The next stage as kids grow older is the evolution of some of these childhood friendships that no longer fit into their middle school days. As children evolve and their interests change, schedules and commitments vary and time is limited, so socializing takes on a new look. This could be the first time your child might be letting go of an old family friend because they no longer see them or want to affiliate with them. Processing these transitions with a conversation about how this experience is feeling is important. For some they are the friend leaving, while others are the friend being left. Either way this is a necessary transition to experience to learn that friendships have a beginning, a middle, and, at times, an end. Remind them that they have love and support at home that will always be there for them.

Message: Making friends can be hard, keeping friends can even be harder, and losing friends can be very difficult. Investing in friendship is a risk for anyone who becomes vulnerable and willing to be available to share and be close to another person outside their family. Support your child in this venture and remember they need your help and guidance as they embark on this very important life skill.

Survival Tip 12:

Teach Your Kids to Play Nice

No one wants their kid to be THAT kid.

On some level, every parent I've ever met is either consciously or unconsciously stressed about getting a note sent home from their kid's teacher that says, *I'd like to schedule a conference with you at your earliest convenience.* And while I certainly can't guarantee that you won't need to have some kind of conversation about your kid's behavior somewhere down the line, the likelihood that your kid is going to get tossed out of public school for not playing nice is low. Very, very low.

Realistically speaking, playing nice and getting along can be a legitimate challenge for some kids. (Let's face it, it can be a challenge for a lot of grown-ups too.) And learning to find our way in a world that's filled with all sorts of new people and new surroundings can be tricky, especially for kids. Though kindergarten attendance is not likely at risk, while teaching your kid to play nice is vital, it's also challenging.

It's important for parents to remember that learning how to successfully interact as a member of a class is one of the main purposes of school. (You didn't actually think it was about learning stuff, did you?)

I mean, it's not easy to control yourself when you're a five- or six-year-old and you've just been thrown into a new and intimidating environment with a bunch of strange classmates for the first time. For almost the whole day. Every day of the week. (Oh yeah, and everybody's parents are gone too.) Just like it's not always easy for older, middle-school-age kids to practice being kind and inclusive because kids that age get sidetracked by things like popularity, ego, or a fear of rejection.

In some cases, those first few weeks of school are a horror show for kids. Because leaving home every day and going off to a place with all new faces and lots of different kinds of new rules, where parents aren't around to reinforce good behavior, is a lot for some kids to handle. A real lot. So, it's no surprise that some of them give the kids around them attitude or aren't inclusive or tease them.

Remember, being nice involves a lot more than just saying *please* and *thank you*. Being nice, at any age, means being self-aware and trustworthy, as well as being able to effectively communicate and collaborate with the kids (or people) around you. And being nice also means being able to get along with people who are different from you.

Being nice involves a lot more than just saying *please* and *thank you*.

You just need to keep it together and not freak out when your daughter has trouble mingling with everyone around her. Or when her teacher tells you she's been a little anti-social. Or when she comes home from school and says she hates everyone in her class. Because it's all perfectly normal.

> 🛋 **When a child's behavior is getting your attention, whether it's bad, good, or indifferent, it is because they are communicating something and quite often unaware of what they are actually trying to say. As parents, it is a very difficult job to try and understand what indeed our child is trying to convey.**

What If My Kid Gets Sent to the Principal's Office, and Other Awkward Encounters

You've gotta trust me here, plenty of kids have trouble with the transition into school, so your kid is by no means a freak if he's fidgety or he can't keep his hands to himself or his teacher says he's having trouble sharing. It happens. And you, as the parent, have to just consistently reinforce the difference between good behavior and bad behavior and what's appropriate and what's not okay. And, eventually, it will take.

As parents sending our kids off to school each day, it can be incredibly nerve wracking worrying about them keeping their behavior in check and not annoying their teacher or the other kids around them. And that doesn't stop when they get older. We never stop worrying about how our kids are going to represent themselves (and us) as they move out into the world. When they start working part-time jobs and interacting with other parents and coaches and the rest of the world at-large, without us at their six, it's always a little stressful worrying about how that's going to go. Like will they be respectful when they're talking to adults? Will they be polite? Will they embarrass themselves (or us)? Or will they access all the things we've taught them and make us proud? And honestly, the answer is *yes* to all of it.

That's why it's important to stay realistic and expect that your kid is going to screw up. She's going to say the wrong thing and do the wrong thing and behave badly in some way, shape, or form. Guaranteed. And usually at the worst possible times.

Stay realistic and expect that your kid is going to screw up.

We don't spend each day in class with them for the first half of the year while they get acclimated, poking them in the ribs when they say or do something wrong. We drop them off on the first day of school and we leave. But in most cases they figure out the dos and don'ts before too long. And the way we ensure that our kids know how to behave with the kids around them is to teach them all those being nice skills at home.

Patterned after EducationAndBehavior.com, here are some simple ways to improve your child's behavior:

- **Verbally acknowledge children's efforts.** Tell your child specifically what he/she did that you are proud of. For example, you can say, "You were so sweet to ask the new girl on your soccer team to go out for ice cream after practice. I'm sure she really appreciated you including her and giving her the chance to connect with the other girls on the team." Or "That was so nice the way you helped your brother with his math homework. He was really struggling." Or "I saw that you shoveled Mrs. Green's walkway after you finished ours. That was a super-thoughtful thing to do because she lives alone." When children get praised for doing the right thing, they want to do more of it.

- **Use positive body language to show approval for positive behavior.** Positive body language can include a smile, thumbs up, or high five.
- **Remind your child that they should be proud of themselves.** When they're not vibing playing on the soccer team but they stick with it 'til the season ends, or when your tween daughter comes to you on her own and asks if she can start babysitting because she wants to earn money on her own, tell them they are awesome. This helps build internal confidence in them, so they can learn to be proud of themselves for being persistent, working hard, being kind to others, et cetera.
- **Take an interest in your child's interests.** Ask them what they enjoy, get excited about their creations or accomplishments, ask them what they want to learn about, and ask them their opinion about things.
- **Acknowledge your child's feelings with empathy.** Be understanding when they're nervous because they're trying something for the first time, frustrated because a writing assignment is difficult for them, disappointed because they didn't get invited to a party, or embarrassed. Avoid saying things like "Stop making a big deal about it," or "Why are you having such a hard time with this; it's easy." Instead, make empathetic statements like, "I understand that you are nervous, that's common when trying something new." Also, let them know that you are there to help in any way you can.
- **Be open-minded and don't pass judgment on your children if their thoughts, values, feelings, or ideas don't match yours.** It's okay to share your opinion, but, in general, don't make them wrong for having their own opinion. They need to feel like they can be open and be themselves around the adults in their lives. When kids feel like they won't be made to feel like they're wrong, they're more likely to talk to us when there's a real problem.
- **Be a role model for good behavior.** If you want your child to treat others with respect, you do the same. If you want your child to be an honest person, set an example of honesty for them.[17]

All of us, moms and dads alike, have spent the last bunch of years devoted solely to raising our kids to be decent, kindhearted little people who'll get along with everyone and toe the line. The blunt reality is, none of our kids can be expected to toe the line 100 percent of the time. We just have to cross our fingers and say a little prayer that they do it the majority of the time.

And that's the thing about those early years in school; this is the first real time in our child's life when they're supposed to start figuring stuff out for themselves. (Emphasis on the word *start*.) They're *supposed* to fall out of trees and spill off bikes and learn what it feels like to be chosen last for the dodgeball team. They're *supposed* to learn that it's not okay to poke someone in the ribs just because they can't have the green crayon. They're *supposed* to figure out how to sit next to someone new instead of sitting next to their best friend at the lunch table. They're *supposed* to figure out that telling secrets about their friend while she's standing directly in front of them, looking them squarely in the face, is not okay. And more often than not, they're going to find this stuff out by doing it the wrong way first, AKA learning it the hard way.

Of course, working in a classroom for over a decade, I've witnessed some pretty extreme cases of kids not being able to deal with being in a mainstream classroom. I've seen everything from biters and hitters and pokers to kickers and spitters and pinchers, and everything in between. I've listened, as kids barely as high as my waist, screamed swear words that would embarrass even a lifelong merchant marine. And I've watched a kid run down a hallway and rip every piece of artwork down without breaking his stride (while screaming obscenities, of course). You get my point.

But you need to remember that most of those kinds of examples are unique situations where a child has a diagnosed behavioral issue that requires either a one-on-one aide to monitor them while they're in a classroom or a different classroom setting altogether. This isn't the norm. I say again, *this isn't the norm.* Besides, if your kid's behavior is that severe that it requires intervention, then you can rest assured that someone on the administrative side is probably going to intervene.

For the majority of parents whose kids are doing typical kid stuff like squirming all over the rug during morning meeting, not keeping their hands to themselves, and talking out during read aloud, this is surprisingly normal behavior. Like the boy in my third-grade class who just couldn't manage to keep his fingers out of his nose. The kid literally left a trail of boogers everywhere he went. And while it was disgusting to those of us who shared a classroom with him, it was totally normal behavior and very short-lived. Within a matter of weeks, he gradually did it less and less because we reacted to it less and less. We told him it was inappropriate behavior and explained that no one wanted to be around him if his fingers were in his nose up to his wrist. Then we ignored it. And the ignoring it was what did the trick. Because since he wasn't getting a reaction from anyone anymore, he lost interest in doing it at all.

When you're up at 2 a.m., lying in bed in a cold sweat over the fact that your daughter doesn't transition well from recess to circle time, you have to consider the fact that she's still a kid and that's one of the things she's in school to learn. So instead of stressing over it, when she's home offer your daughter a series of early warnings before she needs to move from one activity to another. Get her used to a five-minute warning, then a two-minute warning, and so on before she needs to move from one activity to another. Make sure you're giving her positive reinforcement when she transitions smoothly. And the same goes for your older kids who don't manage their transitions well, like from their phones to homework or from homework into the shower and from the shower to bed. Break down what they need to do into manageable steps so what's ahead of them isn't so intimidating.

The thing to keep firmly in mind is that all of these kids meshing together under one roof are coming from all different types of environments, with different rules and different expectations. Some kids are coming at all this as the only child (like I did) or as the older sibling or the middle brother or the younger sister. Some are coming from homes with one dad and no mom or two dads or one mom and no dad (also like me). And as all these little guys migrate from life under their family's roof to the brave new world of school, they have roughly zero transition time. The problem is, it takes time to figure out what behavior is acceptable and what behavior just won't fly. It takes time for kids to learn that they can't talk to their classmates at school in the same way they do to their brother in the privacy of their shared bedroom.

Behavior on the Field Matters Too

It's the same way with competition and good sportsmanship at that age. When most young kids are put in a competitive situation, they're trying to win. Because at that age, games and competition are mostly black and white. They're about winning and losing and not much else. They're young kids who are just starting to learn that there's so much more to competition than winning and losing. But when they're just starting out, the sportsmanship aspect or the being part of a team piece or the confidence-building part are just too much for many of them to grasp. So that's why we tend to see healthy amount of fits and temper flare-ups when they're at recess or in gym class or on their first youth soccer team and something does not go as they would like.

And believe me, I've seen crazy outbursts on places like the soccer field that you'd have to see to believe. Like the middle school girl who felt like she wasn't getting enough playing time so she took off her cleats and threw them at her coach. Bad, very bad. Or the seventh-grade girl who was too overcome by losing a game that she couldn't stop crying long enough to shake hands with the opposing team. Or the sixth-grade boy who threatened to walk off the basketball court because the referee made a bad call.

What we have to do in those situations is remind our kids that there's a code of conduct that we all have to follow when we are in a group or play on a team. Each of us needs to respect everyone on the court or the field or the rink, and that includes our opponents and teammates and our coaches. If our kids aren't capable of that kind of respect, then it's our job to sit them out and help them reflect on their behavior and explain to them that everyone on their team deserves equal courtesy. Whether we are in the car, at the restaurant, or on the basketball court, it's our job to use every teachable moment that we can to teach life lessons. Like when we see another player behaving badly, we need to point that out to our kids as an example of what not to do. Even more impactful, when we see another player behaving well, we need to point that out to our kids so they see what to do.

Remind kids that there's a code of conduct that we all have to follow when we are in a group or play on a team. It's really mostly about simple respect.

🛋 **Children need to understand that there are times to be creative individuals and times to conform to rules and expectations. It is really about learning to work together and creating community.**

What about at Home Can I Relax Behavior Standards?

Now we've talked about how we expect our kids to behave at school and with coaches and at extracurriculars, but what about the one place where it matters most? Home. It's true what they say, that we often don't see who our kids really are, because they're different at home than they are out in the real world. But as true as that statement can often be, it also shouldn't really be that way at all. We need to reinforce with our kids that it's just as important that they follow our rules at home in the same way they do when they're everywhere else. And the way we do that is by explaining what your expectations are and why.

For instance, your kids have been taught that certain voices need to be used in certain places, like libraries and classrooms and stores, to name a few obvious ones—because it's unfair to the people around them if someone's yelling and screaming and being offensively loud. The same applies at home—we can't just run screaming through the kitchen out of respect for the people we live with every day. This is exactly what we tell them when we set the expectation. We explain it like that so it's reasonable and it makes sense to them. Because when we explain the common-sense logic behind the rules we set, our kids can connect with it in a way that feels real and legit, not just something we made up to torture them. And that ensures that they're much more apt to toe the line. Saying that we need to be respectful of the people around us because some places are where people work or study or learn, shows that our kids know that our rules have purpose and aren't just random.

Explain the common-sense logic behind the rules we set so our kids can connect with the rules in a way that feels real and legit.

The same goes for other behaviors, like backtalking or fighting with their siblings or tattling or doing things without asking first. We've got to lay down the expectation in a clear and non-negotiable way so our kids know we mean business. Guide them into understanding why these rules need to be followed everywhere and not just outside in the general population. Explain that something like tattling is what we do when we're just trying to hang someone out to dry. Instead, teach your kids the difference between telling you something important that might be hurtful or dangerous that their brother is doing, instead of just trying to throw them under the bus out of spite. Model the kind of language you expect back from them by using it yourself when you're together. Give your kids some language to help them avoid fighting with their sister. Suggest that they *ask* versus *tell* their sister to give them a chance to pick the TV channel. Or encourage your kids to respect each other by asking permission to wear each other's clothes, instead of just raiding closets. Remind your kids that tiny, but powerful language like "please" and "thanks" go a looooong way toward avoiding fights.

It just makes good sense that learning to behave well needs to start in the home where kids spend most of their time (at least for their first years). If they can be nice at home, they can play nice at school. Of course, everything takes practice. And our kids are at least as imperfect as we are.

> 🛋 **One of the greatest gifts we can give our children is to learn how to deal with differences. As a child we learn to deal with a conflict from those around us. Teaching and modeling some effective communication will help prevent our children from getting into arguments and having meltdowns.**

So if you're getting back comments in your kid's progress report like *Needs Improvement* under the *Demonstrates Self-Control* category or *Unsatisfactory* in the *Plays Well with Others* column, don't immediately start filling out applications for boarding school. Because plenty of kids struggle with these social skills in the beginning.

Just try not to stress too much about how your kids are interacting with people when they're just starting out in school because they're going to screw up, make mistakes, and embarrass themselves (and you) on a regular basis. That's a guarantee. Keep things in perspective and remember that they're still kids with a very underdeveloped social capacity. Expecting them to have perfect manners and behavior and people skills right out of the womb just isn't realistic. These things are all learned—learned from us and their teachers and the world around them. But it takes time.

We eventually learned how to play nice, and so will our children. So just keep reinforcing the good behavior and calling them out on the bad stuff and, sooner or later, it will all click. Ultimately the pushing and shoving and the tattling and backstabbing you see most often during the middle and high school years will stop. And while I know, at this point in the game, you're seeing no end in sight, my now-adult kids and all their former menacing friends are living, breathing proof that I speak the truth. Just hang on. Because like all nauseating and traumatizing amusement park rides you've ever been on, they do eventually level out. Just like this joy ride will. I promise.

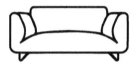

From the Couch of
Debra Fox Gansenberg MSW, LICSW

When a child's behavior is getting your attention, whether it's bad, good, or indifferent, it is because they are communicating something and quite often unaware of what they are actually trying to say. As parents, it is a very difficult job to try and understand what indeed our child is trying to convey.

Tip: Kids don't often have the words to express their feelings, so watching their non-verbal cues and communication is key when trying to understand your child.

Tip: How many times have you had to ask a coworker to repeat what they are asking because you didn't understand? Remember, it is okay to ask your child to repeat or try again when it comes to sharing or trying to explain something. Tell them what you think they said to clarify the information they are trying to share—this shows them that you are listening and care. When a child feels heard, their need to act out and melt down is much less because they are feeling heard and understood.

Tip: Have you ever seen your child trying to sit in a chair for longer than a few minutes? Do they fidget, fall on the floor, or even end up under it? If you have multiple kids, do you have one that just seems to forget what he's supposed to be doing and ends up wandering around aimlessly without a clue? These types of behaviors could be age appropriate, but as they grow older, behaviors like this should resolve. If this is not your experience and your child is in need of several cues and constant redirection, it might be time to explore and gain more perspective about his/her behavior. Your child's behavior could be communicating he is feeling challenged and in need of assistance to master this skill. Knowing when to get professional help is important. When your child's behavior negatively impacts the progress of their day, consider getting some support. There are lots of tools to measure behaviors to better understand their process and find if there is a learning or behavior issue that might need professional attention.

Message: Trying to help kids learn to communicate effectively, behavior appropriately, and understand exactly what they are trying to communicate is a tall order for any mom or dad. Keep it simple, use humor, and don't try and do it all by yourself!

Whether we are in the car, at the restaurant, or on the basketball court, it's our job to use every teachable moment that we can to give life lessons. Children need to understand that there are times to be creative individuals and times to conform to rules and expectations. It is really about learning to work together and creating community.

Tip: When we ask kids to conform, we are simply asking them to follow rules in order to guide their interactions with others. Society isn't asking your kids to push aside who they are with their own special twist. Encouraging kids follow the standards being asked is just going to help them have success in the team, class, or experience at hand. If your child is not able or interested in meeting the expectations of their class or team, they run the risk of peer pressure and rejection, which can be harmful to their own self-esteem. Help enforce social norms and expectations in a restaurant, concert, or sporting event. "Jack, please sit down so that the people behind you can also see the

136

game." Or "Tyler, I need you to put the volume down on your iPad or put it away. We are at a restaurant and the people next to us don't need to be disturbed."

Tip: There are many social norms that our society sets. As parents, you are the ones to pick and prioritize which norms are the ones you want to enforce and follow as a family. Keep in mind your child and his/her capabilities. Are you asking your child to do something that he might not be capable of due to his age, developmental stage in life, or personal challenges? Take the time to make good decisions about where and when you are going to enforce the social expectations as it is your job to set your child up to succeed. If you head out to dinner at seven o'clock with a young child who has not napped and is over-hungry, what are the chances he/she will be capable of meeting the behavioral expectations of sitting in a restaurant? If your child is rather shy and has trouble navigating adults he/she might not know, be careful not to overwhelm your child by requiring him/her to shake each adults' hand and give eye contact if they are not in a great space to do so. Be realistic, make good judgements, and support your child to conform when he/she is ready and capable.

One of the greatest gifts we can give our children is to learn how to deal with differences. As a child, we learn to deal with conflict from those around us. Teaching and modeling some effective communication will help prevent our children from getting into arguments and having meltdowns.
How do you look when you get upset while dealing with conflict? Do you yell? Shut down? Put your hand up to stop the conversation? There are better ways of processing a difference of opinion, but Mom and Dad, we need to get our bad habits to step back because our children are watching. If you scream, they scream; if you slam the door, so will they.

Tip: When we get louder it is because we don't feel heard or validated. In order to prevent slamming doors, yelling, and cursing, we need to stop our misbehavior and start listening. If you watch a disagreement get louder, it is because no one is listening, they are too busy thinking and formulating their rebuttal. So, in fact, you are not being heard because the same thing will happen to you when the other person is processing while you are speaking. The solution: Stop and listen to each other first. Try to reflect back what you heard the other person saying. After each of you has spoken, you will mostly likely feel heard so the voices won't rise.

Tip: A great way to help your kids learn how to have an effective conversation is to practice. One widely used tool is called the ASSERT Formula.

Here's how the ASSERT Formula works:

A: *Approach* the other person you need to speak with and get their attention.

S: Keep it *Simple* while you tell them what you think or how you feel. Keep it short because they will stop listening if you go on too long. "Judy, I need to chat with you; is this a good time?"

S: Discuss the *Specific* behavior. What did the person do to upset you and be specific about the behavior that upset you most. "It has to do with what happened at recess today when you laughed at me."

E: Discuss the *Effect* it had on you. Express the feelings you have as a result of the person's behavior. "I felt really sad when you laughed at me at recess in front of my friend, it was really embarrassing."

R: Explain your reason for wanting to work it out and talk. Reflect how the situation has made you feel. Wait for a *Response* from the other person to see what they have to say. "Well, I didn't mean to embarrass you; sorry."

T: Give a *Term* for how you would like to leave things. Suggest a solution to the problem. "If this happens again, I will have tell the teacher," or "If you keep laughing at me, I am no longer going to play with you at recess."[18]

Tip: Tolerating difference is something that can be hard for just about anyone. The way to begin to navigate this is to simply expose your kids to differences and help them understand you don't have to agree to respect others. It is also important that we don't participate in jokes or other disrespectful behavior that would hurt others who might be different from ourselves. Another way to combat these issues it to nurture esteem in yourself and others so that you are not threatened by difference and can better navigate your own point of view.

Message: Just remember your children are watching you. If resolving conflicts and tolerating differences is a challenge for you, take some time to work at it so that your children don't repeat this legacy. It is not unusual for cultures and points of view to be handed down to us generationally. You can break the cycle and learn and teach new ways of managing significant difference or conflict.

Your Kid Will Grow Out of the Jekyll-and-Hyde Phase Eventually

Our kids do become decent people, regardless of how they start out. So hang in there.

If you feel like your kid is acting a lot like Dr. Jekyll and Mr. Hyde, you're not alone. Kids flip from one mood to another to another to another with the fluidity of a synchronized swimmer, usually without even taking a breath.

Our kids are sweethearts and savages, lunatics and pussycats, all smooshed into one cute little body. And this *multiple-personality syndrome*, as I call it, lasts a while. Sometimes it lasts through the grammar school years and then peaks in middle school, and can even pop up periodically in the high school years. It depends on the kid, really. The one thing we have to remember—even when it seems like they'll never evolve—is that they do, eventually, settle into a groove. They do, eventually, come into their own.

Grammar School Is a Breeze (Well, Kinda)

For the younger kids—the ones in grammar school—their moods and behaviors can change so spontaneously because, for the first time in their lives, they're spending a good chunk of their day at school and away from home—and us. And that can be super stressful for a kid. At school, they're interacting with different people, in a different setting, with different rules and demands, and that can be challenging.

So you might see your kids hitting or kicking or pushing or having trouble sharing, but those are actually pretty normal behaviors for six-year-olds. They're still learning boundaries and good behavior, and they're very much a work in progress. It's our job to coach them when they're home on our turf, so we can reinforce positive behaviors that will carry over when they're in school. In fact, positive reinforcement is one of the best tools we have in our pocket and it's the one we need to use the most.

> 🛋 Being a student is a full-time job of growing, devel-
> oping, and getting involved with activities, exploring
> interests, and making friends to name a few. Navigating
> all this while figuring out what Mother Nature is doing to
> you is quite a task.

Positive reinforcement is one of the best tools we have in our pocket.

A great example is how our youngest, Libby, started out as the most even-keeled kid, never really swinging too high or too low, and then she slowly morphed into a tween who was happy one minute and literally unhinged the next. She went from being unflappable most of the time to slamming doors, acting snarky, and pushing everyone's buttons. God forbid one of us ask her to clean her room. Not a good scene.

The irony is that now, close to a decade later, Libby's settled back into that easy-going girl. Her personality ebbed and flowed through lots of different versions of the same original kid and ultimately came back around to the basic personality she started with. That's who she always was at heart. And that's what tends to happen when kids grow up and mature (key word is *mature*).

To be honest, the only thing that really helped was time. And that's what I've come to learn is the real equalizer. Our kids don't always realize how unreasonable and ridiculous they're acting just because we point it out to them. When our kids are younger, they're often more inclined to toe the line because they haven't started asserting themselves yet. We're still looked at as the authority figures and that tends to carry a little more weight. But once they hit middle school and start getting a taste of independence, they start to separate from us little by little. At the same time, they're also trying super hard to fit in with the kids around them. That's usually around the time they start believing that they know all the answers and begin to give us some push-back. So pointing out how irrational they're being can sometimes be a bad move. They almost always have to become self-aware on their own. And that takes time.

In the meantime, just try to remember that all of the new behaviors you're seeing from your teen, like eye rolling and shrugs and short tempers, are all part of how the teen brain evolves. There's a lot going on in their heads and bodies all at once, and they don't always know the right way to deal with all of the changes—hence the attitude.

Even though the battles we fight when our kids are younger are sometimes a little easier to manage, mood changes are still tricky at any age. I used to see it in my elementary school classrooms all the time, these sweet little girls would play beautifully for 90 percent of recess, and then someone would snap because their piece of sidewalk chalk broke in half. Whether it was someone flipping a switch and melting down because they didn't want to share the jump rope or someone grabbing a fistful of someone else's hair because they wanted a turn on the monkey bars. These sudden and extreme changes in temperament are everywhere when you're dealing with young kids.

Boys slamming a bat on the ground because they struck out. Or girls being overdramatic and reduced to tears because they weren't allowed to join the four-square game. It's everywhere and it's normal—albeit annoying and ridiculous. And that's what we have to keep in mind.

Until they grow up and develop what will eventually be their adult personality, our kids are sampling tons of different behaviors and traits until they find the ones they like best. It's kind of like window shopping—they're just quietly observing. And most of the time they're doing it subconsciously. The point is, at this age, our kids simply lack the capacity to keep themselves in check a lot of the time. Like when Riley, my oldest, and her friend Alex decided it would be funny to lock all the parents out of Alex's house when they were in second grade—incredibly stupid decision. Totally not cool. And certainly not something we thought they'd ever do.

They were having a playdate and they were having fun, so they weren't ready to say good-bye quite yet (typical of most good playdates). It was getting late and we needed to get home for dinner, so we gave the kids the five-minute warning and headed outside to chat on the front porch. The kids snuck downstairs and locked the front door. Needless to say, the looks on our faces must've been classic when we tried the doorknob and realized we were locked out. Then they ran and hid in the playroom, way up in the loft upstairs, so they couldn't even hear us yelling to them to unlock the door. Totally out of character for both of them. But that's just the stuff kids do when they're young. They push buttons and test limits and act on raw impulse.

Eventually the kids came downstairs and we persuaded them to open the door. Both of them knew instantly when they saw our faces that they had crossed a line into a dark place of disobedience. That was consequence enough, because our fear and annoyance scared the crap out of them. So as most parents do when we rescue our kids from a potentially dangerous situation, we focused more on the fact that they were safe and sound and hadn't lit the house on fire than on the bonehead move of locking us out of the house. No real harm, no real foul with a first-time offense.

A teachable moment like that is valuable because we can use it to show our kids what *not* to do and why their behavior is either dangerous or hurtful. That's why we need to sit our kids down while the memory is fresh and explain how their behavior made us feel or how they could've gotten hurt. And in our case, we sat both kids right down and told them how worried and upset we were that we were locked out of the house and didn't know what they were doing on the other side of the door. We explained that there are dangerous things inside the house, like the stove or kitchen knives or prescriptions in the medicine cabinet, that could hurt them and that we were really scared they could get hurt. Believe it or not, they both felt awful about locking us out once they saw how genuinely worried we were. Needless to say, neither of them ever locked anyone out of the house again.

> 📖 **Now, more than ever before, parents are taking a much larger role in finding ways to help children learn life skills. A teachable moment is an opportunity where your child is more receptive to learning a concept because the environment is less formal and an easier place to learn, like while out on a walk or playing at the park.**

The key is not to freak out when your kid does something wrong. Just take a breath and know that kids are going to do all kinds of things that will be frustrating and drive you crazy. Just wait it out, have patience, show them love, and hold to the boundaries you've set. Then give your kids a consequence that fits the crime. Like if they're obsessing over their cell phone at the dinner table, the logical consequence is to remove the phone from the equation.

> **When your kid does something wrong, wait it out, have patience, show them love, and hold to the boundaries you've set.**

Or when your daughter comes home from a playdate with a girl who has, shall we say, a different code of conduct in her family. Like maybe she's allowed to be a little bossy or she's a little spoiled or maybe a little fresh. Then, all of a sudden, you're sitting around the dinner table with your daughter and she barks at you to get up and get her some more milk. And you're like, *wait, what?!* The easiest way to handle the situation is to have a mature conversation with your her, reminding her what the expectation is for behavior in your family. Then explain that if she disrespects you it won't be tolerated.

Aside from their genetic code and some hereditary tendencies and traits, kids come out of the womb pretty much a clean slate—like an empty bowl waiting for ingredients. And every interaction, every word they hear from the second they're born, blends together, kind of like cookie dough. Ultimately, they form something sweet and irresistible.

Here are some solid, practical tips for encouraging good behavior in your kids:

- Reinforce positive behavior by praising your kids for their good behavior. Acknowledge their effort so they'll be more inclined to keep behaving well.
- Model the behavior you expect from your kids by treating them the way you want them to treat others.
- Explain to your kids how their negative behavior is affecting you, like why what they said or did hurt your feelings or upset you.
- Listen to your kids and let them tell you how they feel.
- Teach your kids how to calm down when they get worked up or

frustrated. Encourage them to find a quiet place to go where they can step away from whatever's working them up and regroup.

Tween Drama Is Rough but It Doesn't Last Forever

📔 **They cry, we console them . . . we ask questions, they don't know the answers. Hormones are pretty powerful, and tweens don't know what's happening.**

Even the most mild-mannered kids have their moments. And that's because, as they grow into their adolescent and teen years, they start to wrestle with puberty. Adolescents struggle with all sorts of new relationships and develop what seems like four hundred different personalities all rolled into one unapproachable body.

My suggestion to you at this point is to find a comfy seat, buckle in tight—like airplane tight—and hang on. 'Cause this is where things start to roll upside down. They will roll back. I promise. Because that's exactly how life was in our house when our girls both hit grade school.

Find a comfy seat, buckle in tight—like airplane tight—and hang on.

Now granted, our daughters are three years apart, so we were almost always guaranteed to have one stable kid and one lunatic. And then, of course, it almost always flip-flopped: once one of them hit solid ground, the other one went nuts. But that's just par for the course with kids. As soon as we get even the slightest grip on things, the ground shifts under our feet and we fall into a big, ugly sink hole. Then we climb out and repeat. Over and over and over again.

The key is to:

- Make sure everyone understands that they need to communicate respectfully.
- Try not to let things like the eye rolls and shrugs get to you.
- Do your best to always keep your cool around your kids. Because if you lose control and feed into a screamfest, everyone's gonna lose their cool.
- Keep a tight grip on your positive attitude, because it's that positivity that's going to carry you through these tricky times.

My oldest daughter, Riley, now in college, was super cautious and reserved when she was little. She always stayed squarely inside her comfort zone with things like sports and school and never aggressively pushed herself beyond what she thought were her limits. She did things at her own pace and never let herself be influenced by what other kids around her were doing.

Skip ahead a little to when she got to high school and mix in all the new people and experiences that she was exposed to, and everything changed. She morphed into this fearless, inspired, confident, and passionate woman. She was driven to experience everything she could at her full capacity. She was motivated by the people around her, and she learned how to finally push beyond her perceived limits. (See, it does happen, but it took time.)

That's the thing about parenting . . . we can't seem to imagine our kids evolving out of the phase they're in right now, but they do. It's hard to imagine that one day they'll be able to follow the rules or talk to us without the snarky attitude or show us the respect we deserve, but it happens. We just need to be relentless in reminding them what our expectations are for their behavior and hold them accountable when they forget. Because remember, they call parenting a *labor of love* for a reason. 'Cause it's not easy, but it's definitely worth the effort when our kids finally get there.

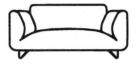

From the Couch of
Debra Fox Gansenberg MSW, LICSW

Being a student is a full-time job of growing, developing, and getting involved with activities, exploring interests, and making friends to name a few. Navigating all this while figuring out what Mother Nature is doing to you is quite a task. Kids are busy doing their job of learning to be more cooperative, conscientious, and follow directions too. One of their biggest challenges while maturing is learning how to express themselves verbally, finding the right words to explain what they are feeling. While they learn these things, oftentimes it comes out sideways and not so pretty; parents, we need to help them figure it out.

Tip: Whether they are in preschool, grade school, middle school, or high school, routine is always important. If kids know when they are to eat, wash, brush, sleep, and wake, chances are they can eventually take control of these things and become more independent. Once they take ownership of their own self-care, then they can eliminate Mom and Dad having to nag and, as a result, there are less altercations and tempers don't flare.

Tip: Finding the perfect resource for your developing child might be just the thing to get them in the know about what is happening to them. Mood swings, zits, periods, pubic hair—it's a lot to make sense of. Providing a book they can read with or without you can provoke wonderful questions and discussion to help kids learn what is coming down the road. We cannot always rely on the school puberty talk—who knows if they will even listen.

Tip: Blame it on biology, mood swings are simply hormonal shifts that are bound to happen during puberty. Irritability, sadness, and frustration are normal occurrences if indeed you are in the throes of pre/adolescence. As a parent, use humor and share your war stories, if they will listen, to help normalize what they are going through. However, it is important to note that if your child's moods interfere with their *everyday* process on a longer-term basis, this could be a sign that this could be a mental health issue worth looking into.

Message: Moms and dads make the most of the up times when you see smiles and hear laughter. These good days balance out the days or even weeks of ups and downs with no predictability in sight. Hold on tight, do a lot of listening, and hold back on judgements and opinions and this, too, shall pass. Remind your kids that all of their various emotions are welcome, just help them learn how to express themselves in ways that you approve of in your home.

Now, more than ever before, parents are taking a much larger role in finding ways to help children learn life skills. A teachable moment is an opportunity where your child is more receptive to learning a concept because the environment is less formal and an easier place to learn, like while out on a walk or playing at the park.

Tip: The keys to a teachable moment are timing and location! Finding a time where you can catch your kids being curious and available to absorb something new can be tricky. Using humor during an unexpected moment can make it feel a little more informal and comfortable. Whether it is at the park, in the tub, or in line at McDonald's, the key is to capture your child's attention long enough for them to learn something in that given moment. "Meg, we are sitting here at the movies and you keep kicking the chair in front of you. How do you think the person sitting in front of you is feeling? Do you think you could apologize now, please?" "JJ, we are sitting in your sister's fort and I see you eating her secret stash of candy without her knowing. How would you feel if she did that to you?"

Tip: Timing and location can be important to a teachable moment, but what can also be impactful is when they are in the presence of another peer. Asking questions, seeking answers, and getting curious together makes a great teachable moment. "Wally, can you tell Mike and Jon how it made you feel when they skipped your turn during our game of Sorry just now?" or "Lisa, you threw down your glove and bat and stormed off. Tara, can you share with Lisa how you felt when she left the game today?" The setting could be anywhere asking these questions, in the dugout, at the conference table, but most important is the process where the learning happens.

Message: Be mindful of the people, place, and process when it comes to a teachable moment. These situations can be less formal, more fun, and a place where the best teaching can happen. If, for some reason, you are sitting with a bunch of quiet clams and it doesn't work, try again, it will work one of these times.

They cry, we console them . . . we ask questions, they don't know the answers. Hormones are pretty powerful, and tweens don't know what's happening.

We need to spend time understanding their physical development and how it is impacting their emotional health. Stressors typically probe at our teens, which then can lead to anxiety, depression, headaches, and more. What we can do is teach or kids how to better manage what is in their control.

Tip: Our preteens are forced to grow up too quickly these days, which can create a sense of rushing through the developmental stages. They are quick to dress in promiscuous fashions, use verbiage fit for an older kid, or even partake in activities more appropriate for a high-schooler. As parents, we need to step in and take some control, helping our kids manage themselves and make good decisions. This can be hard, especially with a strong willed or opinionated teen, so stand firm and don't back down.

Tip: Help kids learn the side effects of puberty, hormones, and maturity. All these things come with a new-found sense of responsibility. If they chose to express themselves by whining, yelling, and lots of tears, help them dial it down and take a step back. Model for them what it looks like to take five and regroup. If you do it, and it helps, maybe they will too. Encourage kids to learn how to meditate using apps on their phone or head to a yoga class to calm their body. Offer to play along and learn as you both head for new territory; it might be nice to experience these things together so your teen doesn't feel so alone.

Tip: Kids this age have so many things they are worrying about: their appearance, academics, and social life. Lots of stressors impact their chemistry. Too much stress hormone can lead to too much adrenaline, which leads to cortisol that can create a hormonal imbalance. Take time to check in with their pediatrician and get a thorough annual check to understand where they are in their development. Knowledge is important when trying to understand your child's behavior when they really don't empathize with themselves.

Message: Growth spurts, sexual maturation, and puberty changes are happening sooner or later for each of your children. Knowing this is coming down the pike, prepare yourself by speaking with a specialist, reading some recent resources, and watching them carefully. During this time, your adolescent is struggling for independence and more control, while at the same time, scared of how it actually might feel to decide for themselves. Watch out for peer influence, romantic relationships, and your teen's new challenges. Prepare for all sorts of outcomes, whether it be smiles and hugs or tears and tantrums. Brace yourself, remain calm, and arm yourself with your own support system to see you through this part of the journey.

Survival Tip 14:

There's No Way Around Drama ... So Learn to Be Zen about It

The calmer and more level-headed you are when drama happens, the better off everyone will be in the end.

Drama. Just the single, stand-alone word is enough to make any parent throw up in their mouth. (It's almost as traumatic as the word *lice.* Almost.) Kid drama can pop up any time, without any warning, without any real rhyme or reason, and it can be debilitating, sucking the life out of us and our kids. Not to mention that it's often tricky to resolve. It's important, as a parent, to be able to keep it all in perspective, so we ensure that our kids learn to do the same.

It doesn't matter how well-adjusted or easygoing our kids are, drama happens. It just does. It's doesn't discriminate either. It affects everyone, regardless of their social status or gender or age. How we address it and how we teach our kids to deal with it, though, can make all the difference in terms of everyone surviving it.

Prep Yourself for Two Basic Types of Drama

As far as the types of drama we're likely to see in elementary and middle school go, we're mainly talking about two categories. You've got your **friend drama** and your **home drama**, two decidedly different varieties. Both can be dicey.

Broken down into simplest terms, friend drama involves any kind of conflict our kids have with other kids. But you knew that. It includes, but isn't limited to, stuff like teasing, bullying, and being excluded. It can come from the most unlikely places, like the kids we'd never expect. You know, the ones who were our daughter's best friend two days ago. Which is exactly why we've always told our own kids that people will surprise them in the *best* and in the *worst* of ways.

Now I know most young parents don't even consider drama as a viable issue until their kids hit middle school, and why would they? Cute, cuddly little kids don't seem like they have the capacity to be dramatic. It just naturally seems like that's an issue that affects tweens and teenagers. Assuming that drama doesn't touch the littler kids, though, is a big mistake. HUGE. Because let me tell you, it starts way earlier than we'd ever expect, especially once our kids start going to school. When they're spending hours and hours each day with the same people, kids will start to clash, cliques will start to form, and feathers will inevitably get ruffled. I say this not only as the mom of two girls who could never stay out of each other's faces for more than four consecutive minutes, but also as a former classroom aide who saw drama in the classroom on a daily basis throughout my twelve years in the school system.

> Stay calm, listen closely, and remember you don't have to fix it! Parents, we don't have to give our kids a stage for all their drama, sometimes we need to just keep it simple and help them walk away.

Assuming that drama doesn't touch the littler kids is a big mistake. HUGE.

The bizarre thing is that even though everyone is still playing together in a relatively harmonious way early on (the operative word there is *relatively*), the possibility of drama is always lurking *just* under the surface. And it happens like a car crash, in the blink of an eye, when you least expect it.

I've seen third-graders bring other third-graders to tears over everything from what they're wearing to how they smell (yeah, it happened) to how they throw a ball to whether or not they like tuna fish sandwiches (my youngest daughter got that one). Thankfully, by the time they've grown up a little, matured, and realized that saying mean stuff is actually hurtful, they knock it off and everyone's friends again—at least most of the time. And for the record, I've seen middle-schoolers bring each other to tears over the exact same things.

The reality is, bullying is a huge issue and there's a better-than-average chance that your kid(s) are going to encounter it somewhere along the line. Whether they're the victim or the perpetrator or a bystander, it's going to affect them at some point and on some level. I can promise you that watching them go through it is one thousand times worse than anything we may have gone through as a kid. The best thing you can do for your child (and yourself) is to understand how to handle bullying when it happens. And that involves having conversations long before a situation falls in their lap.

We need to arm our kids with the strategies and language they need to help them avoid and avert bullying altogether. Above all, we have to ensure that they respect the people around them—whether they like them or not. Because even though we don't have to like the people around us, we do have to be respectful. After respect, we need to give our kids the language to use with a bully. Teach your kids simple phrases like, "Please stop," "That was unkind," "Please leave me alone," and "If you don't stop, I'm going to talk to the teacher." Then we teach our kids the difference between being a bystander and an *upstander*. We help them avoid being a bystander who just silently watches an incident go down, and we encourage them, instead, to be an upstander and intervene or give assistance when someone's being harassed. Finally, we just keep checking in with our kids. And checking. And checking. And checking, so they know that we're there to support them if they need us.

> 📖 **The bully, the bullied, and the bystander are all important roles to understand in any situation where an individual is being physically or emotionally harmed. Kids need to learn that any one of these roles is just as important to pay attention to as the victim.**

In contrast, home drama, is a whoooooole different animal. Fortunately (or unfortunately) for us, our kids reserve their worst behavior for home or when they're out in public places with their family.

No matter what kind of kid you're raising, no matter how in control and well-adjusted they are, at some point, they all melt down. And once that happens, the drama oozes out like an open head wound. It's like they say: we never truly see our own child the way the rest of the world sees them.

A perfect example is the kid I saw coming through the front doors at school who would never dare open her mouth to me or her teachers but wouldn't hesitate to mouth off to her mom over something like packing room-temperature Gatorade in her lunchbox. (I've seen it. It happened.) As horrifying as it is to watch as a bystander, it's much worse when you're that parent, and the blows are flying—like Bruce Lee's one-inch punch to the chest. The reason for this wildly different behavior is that our kids feel a very different comfort level with family, under their own roof, than they do with the general population. For better or for worse, they feel more comfortable.

This particular Gatorade girl was a piece of work. She was an only child and her mom was totally devoted to catering to her daughter's every ridiculous whim—all the way through middle school. If the daughter was carrying her backpack and had to use another hand to carry a project or a lunchbox, she'd refuse, telling Mom to carry it to class for her. And she wouldn't hesitate to lash out at Mom if other people were around. Didn't matter if a teacher was standing in front of her, or the principal or the guidance counselor, she'd let the demands fly. Freely. Even though most kids reserve their really epically bad behavior for us, in the privacy and comfort of home, there are plenty of kids out there who don't think twice about behaving badly or being rude or disrespectful in public. How we handle outbursts and demands can make us or break us.

If we allow that kind of behavior, then we're enablers. We're to blame for having dramatic, insolent kids. If they're talking to *us* like that, publicly, just imagine what they're saying to their friends and how they're behaving with their teachers and other parents. That's why we need to make sure that we set a clear expectation with our kids early on, so they know that kind of behavior won't be tolerated. This is exactly what Dave and I tried to do from the get-go. Our kids knew that if they crossed a certain line, like talking back to us in public or throwing a fit because we wouldn't let them have something, then there would be consequences. Even though that strategy wasn't always guaranteed, enough reinforcement of that idea over the years helped them grow a healthy desire to behave respectfully. It made enough of an impression, in fact, that whenever they'd see a child grossly misbehaving out in public, they'd cringe and make some kind of a comment about how embarrassed they were for the kid's parents.

If we allow disrespectful behavior, then we're enablers.

As our kids start experiencing drama out in the real world, we need to constantly reinforce the fact that everyone is dealing with emotional growing pains, but not everyone deals with them the same way. Kids are impressionable. Some more than others. We all know that. A lot of kids get sucked into the world of drama because it gives them a feeling of being in control, and they're just not mature enough yet to know that 99 percent of it is a ridiculous waste of time and energy. For them, it's a way to assert themselves and have power over other kids, wrong as that is. Luckily, they do tend to grow out of it—in time. (Just usually not soon enough for us.)

Sometimes, though, drama isn't that cut and dry. Sometimes simple, easily-resolved kid drama, like not being asked to a friend's sleepover or girls being caddy and talking about each other behind their backs, evolves into bullying. And because bullying is such a super-sensitive issue facing today's kids (and parents), it's especially important that we all know how to identify it and, more importantly, what to do when it happens to our kids.

How Do You Tell If It's Kid Drama or Bullying?

In the most basic terms, drama is usually a clash between two or more kids that most often gets resolved by the kids themselves. It can be hurtful and annoying, sure, but it can generally be handled between the kids and without getting parents or teachers involved. But bullying, that's on a totally different level. When a kid uses words or actions that are *specifically* designed to intimidate another kid, that's classic bullying. And as soon as your son or daughter is confronted with that kind of behavior on a recurring basis, it's time for parents to intervene.

What to do when your kid is the one being bullied is a toughy. So here are some tips for surviving that kind of situation:

- Make sure you're listening to your child when they start talking to you about being bullied.
- Do your best to keep your own emotions in check while you're listening to what's gone down; because if your kid sees you getting fired up, that's going to fire them up too.
- Praise your child for coming to talk to you about what's going on and encourage them to also fill in key people at school, like their principal or guidance counselor or teacher. If your child is young or unlikely to report the problem to school, you must advocate for them.
- Remind your child that if talking things out with the kid who's hassling you doesn't get them anywhere, then the next best thing to do is to walk away and tell an adult they trust what is going on.
- Make sure that your child knows not to fight back but instead to walk away and get help.

Prep for Middle School Drama

As our older, preteen kids start spending time together in classrooms and on playing fields and in groups and clubs, the potential for drama grows exponentially. And because preteens are emotionally immature and inexperienced at, you know, everything, stuff that shouldn't be causing problems ends up causing big ones. That's because most kids don't relate well with reason, logic, and common sense. When drama finds them, they're not wired with the capacity to behave rationally. So they often blow things out of proportion and can't rein themselves in. (Hence, the meltdown.)

As parents, the first thing we need to do is understand how the adolescent and teen brain works. Because once we have a solid understanding of what's going on under the hood, the better equipped we'll be to deal with breakdowns along the way.

Here's the simple explanation of how the adolescent brain works, straight from LiveScience.com. "After infancy, the brain's most dramatic growth spurt occurs in adolescence, and that growth means things get a little muddled in a teen mind."[19] According to StanfordChildren's.org, "the rational part of a teen's brain isn't fully developed and won't be until he or she is twenty-five years old or so."[20] In other words, your adolescent or teen's brain just hasn't made all the necessary connections yet from the back of the brain to the front. But it will, in time. Until then, though, it's our job to help them navigate challenging situations like relationships and peer pressure and stress.

That's why, as the parent of a kid dealing with drama, our most valuable tool is simply helping our kids gain a real perspective on the "crisis." We need to help our kids take a step back and take an honest look at what they're getting so upset about to see if it's really worth all the energy. And while that's *just* about impossible in most cases, we still have to try to redirect all that illogical thinking before it gets the better of them.

Our most valuable tool is simply helping our kids gain a real perspective.

The critical thing to remember when we encounter drama is that *we can't fear it*, as intimidating as it can be. (And it is, believe me.) It's going to happen, whether we're prepared for it or not. We just need to understand, ahead of time, that our kids are going to become totally, oh, I don't know, childish about their friendships and relationships at some point along the line—like crazy-train childish. If we can think of it almost like a natural baptism into the world of being a tween, then it somehow eases the shock of dealing with it day-to-day. They all have their moments, every one of them, when they're confronted with conflict. Learning to deal with it is a life skill that we all need to learn.

Also, since most drama is so irrational and spontaneous to begin with, there's no foolproof way of dealing with it when it happens. Sorry, but that's the reality. It's actually a lot like dealing with a trick birthday candle that keeps relighting—we're never really able to snuff it out. Which is why it's our job as the moms and dads to douse the drama with a firehose if we see it's going too far. Just be sure not to rescue too quickly. Jumping in and getting involved when our kids are in conflict with a friend should be our last resort. Before we go for the assist, we need to back away and let them try to handle the situation on their own. However, if the drama gets physical or they get threatened or make a threat, then we move in quickly, because they're still naïve, inexperienced kids who need our guidance.

Oftentimes, the best thing we can do to help our kids navigate dramatic situations is to encourage them to stay calm, take a step back, and remind them that we're there for them when they need us. Our kids are way more likely to think rationally when we're rational.

Equally as important is that we need to be honest with our kids and point out when *they* are actually the problem. As we all know, there are always two sides to every story, and as much as we'd love to assume that our kids are always angels, they're not. They are human, and they make mistakes and say and do things that they shouldn't, in spite of the best upbringing and guidance. That's why it's important that we call our kids out when we see them acting or sounding mean, either with friends or at home with their own siblings. Make them aware of how powerful their words and actions are. Teach them the kind of impact they can have on someone else's feelings and self-esteem. Encourage them to put themselves in someone else's shoes before they open their mouth.

> **As much as we'd love to assume that our kids are always angels, they're not; they're human, and they make mistakes.**

Now because I have two girls, I don't speak boy. Not a single word. Even our dog is a girl. So I can't really talk too much about the boy side. I can only speak to what I saw when I worked with boys every day in the classroom. And from what I've seen over the years, boy confrontations are decidedly different from girl conflicts, even though both are still emotionally draining, time-consuming, and generally annoying. Boys tend to bottle stuff up and get more physical, while girls tend to be a little drippier with their emotions and play more head games with each other. But both sexes have their challenges.

A classic example is when a bunch of boys are playing what's *supposed* to be flag football and then some kid goes rogue and flying body slams the guy who's got the ball. Happens all the time. Then punches get thrown and someone inevitably ends up in the nurse's office with a bloody nose. Garden variety boy drama. I have a friend whose sixth-grade son and a friend get together almost every day to jump on their trampoline and talk about superheroes. At least once a week, though, this goes south because the boys end up arguing about which hero is the most powerful. It usually ends with her son storming into the kitchen saying he'll never play with his friend again. And my friend just gives her son a snack and listens while he blows off steam. The next day, without fail, one of them goes knocking on the other's door and they're back to being best friends. That's because boy drama is usually pretty straightforward. Boys get mad, they blow up, and then they're over it and sitting around the table together eating tacos like nothing ever happened.

The key with boys is to just listen, encourage them to take a little space from the friend they're having a problem with, and then feed them some chips and salsa.

Girls, though, they're a different breed altogether. Our brand of drama is usually more psychologically based. We get in each other's heads and then destroy each other from the inside out. And it starts early. (I think because girls are just born with dramatic tendencies already wired into our DNA.) Even when they're in the younger grades, I don't know how, they mess with each other's heads. There's the whole crying piece, which doesn't happen nearly as often with boys, and the jealousy factor and the exaggeration factor, that all adds up to an ugly, snotty mess.

So as far as girl drama is concerned, I can probably tell you everything you ever wanted to know, but to sum it up, it sucks. That's just the plain and simple truth. Girls are dramatic by nature, so their responses to emotional situations are almost always going to be amplified. While boys can be angry at each other one minute, they're playing basketball the next. But girls, we tend to hang onto our emotions, almost feeding off them.

It would happen on a daily basis that I'd take a group of fourth-grade girls out to recess and one minute they'd be all lovey-dovey, playing four square and braiding each other's hair, and then, without any warning at all, one of them would collapse in tears. Oftentimes it was because a friend said they couldn't sit together anymore at lunch. Devastating. Then there is the case of the group of sixth-graders who would talk about after-school playdate plans, but one of them wasn't invited. Never a good outcome there. Or when our daughter's new BFF (you know, since yesterday's soccer practice) decides to be someone else's bestie and the trauma is almost too intense to bear.

These little episodes, oftentimes, drag out for what seems like forever. Girls like to drag stuff out and regurgitate the agony and the suffering and the crisis over and over and over, until everyone in the vicinity knows about it and lines have been drawn and sides have been taken. Any girl knows this to be true. Think of girl drama like a carnival mirror that brutally distorts the real image that it's reflecting. That's girl drama. Horribly distorted most of the time.

The unfortunate thing about drama is that so much of it centers on a power struggle. There's almost always that *one boy* or that *one girl* who just dominates everyone else. You know, the Alpha Male and the Alpha Female. We have them in all areas of our life, but the first time we're usually exposed to them is when we're young and in school. I still remember the girl who bullied me through elementary school. Vividly. That kind of drama stays with you.

Social Media Can Fan Drama

Then there's the drama that comes along with social media. That can be a really dicey kind of drama. Because once you give your kid a device like a smartphone or laptop that allows them to connect with tons of other kids, on multiple platforms, on a host of different social networks, you've just completely changed the game. You've plugged them into the world at large on a totally different level. I say it that way because giving kids access to the world of social media means you're allowing them to connect with the entire world around them through the click of a mouse. While that ability to circumnavigate the globe from their phone or their desk is amazing, because it allows them to learn and cultivate interests and grow friendships, it can also be a gateway to scarier things like cyberbullying. And the blowback from that is infinitely worse than one-on-one bullying. In a matter of seconds, a cyberbully can embarrass your kid in front of an entire community.

We have to educate our kids on how to handle themselves online and teach them how to behave and how to protect themselves, so we can keep the drama down to a minimum. By giving them guidelines and teaching them what's okay and what's off limits, we can help them stay safe.

📖 **Gen Zers have never lived life without the internet or social media. The conflict for us is the world of learning and socializing is often done online. How do we keep them cyber safe while we are learning how to navigate our own way?**

I know we've covered a lot of ground here, so now you should have the basic gist of what lies ahead. You should also have a sense of how to handle drama when it happens. You'll play it exactly like you would when your toddler falls off her scooter—you won't flinch until she does. You'll stay calm and not pounce hysterically overcome by the sight of a skinned elbow. You won't react until you see how *your child reacts*. And then, if the trauma is *so* bad that you have to rush over, you'll help calm her down, throw a Band-Aid on her arm and take her for ice cream and then help her climb back on the scooter. But you certainly won't perpetuate the situation by taking and posting pictures of the goriness on Facebook or Instagram so the whole world gets to feed into the drama, because that would be stupid. Right? Right.

It's almost like we have to consider ourselves deputized members of a bomb squad, diffusing every potential explosion *before* it happens. Since we can't cut the right wire every single time, we do have to expect that some dramatic moments will inevitably blow up in our face. Your daughter may get amped up because her BFF didn't share her Cheese Nips at school and you try to explain that she really doesn't have to because it's *her* snack. Your son might get annoyed at his friend because he didn't return his football and you'll remind him that all he needs to do is remind his buddy that he never gave it back. And keep in mind that there will be plenty of times that our explanation, as logical as it is, is useless. Sometimes we just have to wait it out.

Here's the bottom line for how to survive the majority of kid drama that comes our way . . . keep as calm and as rock steady as you can when kids are being dramatic so that we don't fan the fire. Because what happens to a fire when we fan it? It gets all the extra oxygen it needs to grow big and hostile and unruly. That's why we douse it with water instead. And in this case, our calm, Zen-like attitude is like a big sloshy bucket of water.

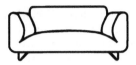

From the Couch of
Debra Fox Gansenberg MSW, LICSW

Stay calm, listen closely, and remember you don't have to fix it! Parents, we don't have to give our kids a stage for all their drama, sometimes we need to just keep it simple and help them walk away.

Helping kids manage their reactions and behavior is important. This is a time in your child's life where we need to help them learn how to regulate their emotions, so that their journey isn't a dramafest.

Tip: Half the battle of beating teen drama is lessening their chance to overreact to a simple situation. Help your kids learn ways to stay calm and not be quick to react. It might help to change the scene of the stressful conversation and help them step away from the scenario for a minute. Deep breathing and relaxing helps before you re-enter the conversation with more of a sense of calm. Talking and listening at a slow pace will help with any impulsive response from your child and prevent any unnecessary drama.

Tip: If you become aware of your child taking part in a highly emotional situation, I would encourage shutting down any social media or phone activity in order step back and take a break. Constant contact makes it very difficult for kids to escape from situations that can be upsetting or stressful. Gen Zers don't know how it feels to be logged off from everything; teach them how unplugging can be really useful, especially during difficult times.

Tip: Parents, find below five tips to teach your kids to avoid teenage drama:

- Pick your friend groups carefully. If there are kids that can be unkind, confrontational, or like to the attention of being trouble-makers, think twice before including them in your social circles or joining theirs.
- Avoid dramatic people; there will be those kids who always have a problem or conflict and need to share it with the whole cafeteria by

loud outbursts or sobbing. When this happens around you, don't make contact or get involved. You don't need others' problems or negativity.

- Avoid gossip, whether it's listening to it or spreading it. If someone is talking to you about another friend, chances are they talk about you behind your back too. If you are asked to participate in any way, head in the other direction.
- Be a trustworthy friend; if people share things with you in confidence, don't become part of the rumor mill. If asked questions or pressured for information, let people know you are being a good friend and choose not to repeat what someone has confidentially shared with you.
- Avoid being pulled into someone else's conflict. You don't want to be involved in the middle of an emotional display.

Message: One thing that hasn't changed in this ever-changing world is teenage drama. It is real, it happens, and it can be a lot for your teen to manage and stay clear of. Listen to your teen, reflect back to them what you understand they are saying, and reassure them you are here to support them.

The bully, the bullied, and the bystander are all important roles to understand in any situation where an individual is being physically or emotionally harmed. Kids need to learn that any one of these roles is just as important to pay attention to as the victim.

Bullying has become a huge buzz word for Gen Zers because bullying has been an epidemic in their lifetime. They have grown up being educated from a young age about the act of harming or intimidating another person to the point of emotional or physical harm. Teaching our kids to recognize bullying, do something about, and manage themselves is just as important.

Tip: A great lesson to teach your kids is that we cannot control anyone, including a bully. What we can do is control our own behavior and reaction. Ultimately, it is up to parents and teachers to help kids learn how to effectively respond to a bully whether they are the victim or bystander.

Tip: Teaching kids what to do to help themselves or someone else is important. Encourage them to SPEAK UP. Tell a teacher, coach, parent, or any adult who can help keep them safe. The offender's parents may need to be notified if the bullying won't stop. If you don't feel comfortable with direct contact, ask administrators or even a police officer to assist in the conversation. Teach your children to walk around a bully and avoid contact or interaction to keep themselves safe. If they see someone being bullied, encourage them to step in if they feel it's safe or run to get help.

Tip: What if your child is the bully? The most important thing to do is listen to whoever is delivering the message that your child is bullying others. No one likes getting the news, but avoid being defensive and listen; every kid is capable of bullying. Engage your child in a dialogue with a guidance counselor or therapist to help learn what your child is trying to communicate, so you can learn what he might need. Another valuable piece here is the repair work after the incident. Use this as an opportunity for your child to learn his/her impact on another and offer an apology. Hopefully a lesson will be learned by taking ownership and accountability for the bullying behavior.

Message: As a youngster, what did you do if you were teased, threatened, or hurt by the neighborhood bully? Did you help the boy being teased at the lunch table, or did you stay quiet? We need to teach our kids how to take control of any situation and help create a successful outcome. Help them understand that doing nothing only teaches the bully they can strike again.

Gen Zers have never lived life without the internet or social media. The conflict for us is the world of learning and socializing is often done online. How do we keep them cyber safe while we are learning how to navigate our own way?
Stepping into our children's cyber world is the first step to understanding and learning how to navigate their safety. The days of meeting your kid's friends at the playground are over; be prepared to be faced with a Snapchat photo or FaceTime call to finally meet the friend your child has been talking about.

Tip: Frankly parents, just make sure you are clothed all the time because when you least expect it you could be spotted on social media first thing on a Sunday morning. Understanding this situation is important; it is a perfect example of how our kids are growing up in a different world than we did. Rules are a must to begin a safe cyber journey. How much time are you okay with them being online? Which sites are they allowed to go on? Are they allowed to have any social media accounts? What are they allowed to post on their social media? These are all first steps to setting limits for your child to handle all this technology. If the rules are not followed, just remember they earned whatever is next. They are showing you that they might not be ready to handle all the technology they have access to, so you might need to just shut it down and try again at another time.

Tip: A great way to enforce cyber safety is the location of the home computer; this is a must for kids prior to carrying a phone on them 24/7. Having kids learning how to navigate their way on the computer and internet can be tricky, so keeping them close enables peeking over the shoulder to help teach and guide your child. A hazard of a newbie is actually coming across content that they were not looking for or prepared to see. Encourage kids to share with you right away if something appears that is not child friendly, such as pornography, rude language, or unwanted contacts.

Tip: A parent favorite is learning how to navigate free parental controls, safe surfing options, and hardware safety products out on the market. Our children are smart and probably know more than we do when it comes to technology. Take a class or take the time to learn about any and every way in your control to protect your child!

Tip: Teach your kids how to protect themselves in cyber space. Help them understand if they don't take precautions than they are possibly going to deal with some awful consequences. Keeping their identity, whereabouts, and personal information offline is important. As they enter the tween and teen years, they will need to understand that sharing passwords and pictures can lead to trouble.

Message: There are lots of lessons to be learned here, and we are responsible for teaching them if we are going to hand our children any sort of technology. Make careful decisions about when you are going to give access, for how long, and what for. Kids are going to get their hands on devices one way or another. Keep their access as a privilege so that someday, when they earn a consequence, it will actually matter. NO screens is the worst!

Survival Tip 15:

Foster a Healthy Sense of Wit and Sarcasm in Your Kids

There are more hidden benefits to having a good sense of humor than you know.

There's nothing worse, in my opinion, than a snarky, loudmouthed kid who makes inappropriate comments and makes you want to pretend that you're not actually her parents. But show me a kid who can really banter with the big boys and understands the fine art of sarcasm and *that's* the one I want to hang with. *That's* the one I'm proud to call my own.

Teaching our kids the difference between being playfully and appropriately sarcastic and being fresh and completely rude is tough. But it *can* be done. And when it's done successfully, it's one of the most charming qualities you'll love about your kids. Because contrary to the old-school philosophy of kids needing to be seen and not heard, allowing and encouraging a child to be witty and playful can enable that child to grow into an adult who can carry themselves in social situations and engage the people around them. And doing it well is a life skill, as far as I'm concerned—**a really valuable life skill**.

Stay with me here and don't panic—testing boundaries through communication and language is totally normal as kids grow and mature. It's just another way our kids are coming into their own.

Let me explain why I feel so strongly about the benefits of raising a child with a healthy sense of sarcasm. But before I do, it's important to clearly define the true essence of sarcasm. First of all, according to my bud Oscar Wilde, "Sarcasm is the lowest form of wit but the highest form of intelligence." So right there you know it's got some teeth.

In simplest terms, and according to *Merriam-Webster*, sarcasm is *"the use of words that mean the opposite of what you really want to say especially in order to be funny."* It is finding irony in the world around us or putting a slight twist on an observation. Now the extended definition includes words like *insult* and *irritation*, but that's not the kind of sarcasm I'm talking about here. What I'm talking about is the kind that's meant to be a harmless, non-offensive joke. Because the last thing I'd suggest is that we teach our kids how to mock other people or convey contempt. That would be bad.

What I *am* suggesting is that there are some hidden benefits to raising a kid who is quick-witted. For example, when mixed with thoughtfulness and self-control, sarcasm can enhance your child's creativity because they're forced to think more abstractly. In other words, it stimulates the creative thinking process. Not to mention that they have to be able to process their exchanges with people much faster than in regular conversation.

There are studies that support the idea that sarcastic people are more creative than non-sarcastic types. Yep. It's true. In Eric Fluckey's *Huffington Post* article, "Why Sarcasm Is So Great," he wrote, "scientists from Harvard, Columbia, and INSEAD Business School were curious if sarcasm had any effects on a person's cognitive abilities. So they decided to run a little experiment." (Love that that's what they spent their time and resources evaluating.) These scientists concluded, "the people in the test groups who had given or received sarcastic remarks in conversations outperformed those who didn't. In fact, they were found to be about three times more creative." Because, Fluckey says, "both the giver and the receiver had to mentally work out the contradictory nature of sarcasm for it to be effective. The mental processes involved in the interpretation and delivery seems to flame the creative spark."[21]

Remember, at our core, human beings are social animals. Most of us thrive on contact and communication with other people. Because of that, our society has evolved into a culture of quick thinkers. Believe it or not, the *Smithsonian* magazine actually says, "Children understand and use sarcasm by the time they get to kindergarten."[22] It's our responsibility as parents to raise kids who can keep up, intellectually, with the people around them. We need to kindle their sense of humor early on so they can understand and benefit from how humor and sarcasm play in the world they're growing up in.

In today's culture, raising a kid who can survive and thrive in a world where sarcasm has become mainstream is essential. And I can actually back that up, thanks to John Haiman, a linguist at Macalester College in Minnesota, who agrees that "sarcasm is practically the primary language in today's society."[23] Yeppers, it's true. So in an effort to prepare our kids to be able to successfully engage in today's competitive world, they need to be fluent banterers and pack a well developed sense of humor.

According to KidsHealth.org, "a good sense of humor is a tool that our kids will rely on throughout life." They say "kids with a well-developed sense of humor are happier and more optimistic, have higher self-esteem, and can handle differences (their own and others') well."[24] And in my experience, both as a mom and as an educator, they're right.

Some of the most well-adjusted kids (and adults) I know have an incredible sense of humor. As far as I'm concerned, it just adds to their charm. They know how to make people laugh and think and feel at ease. Some of my favorite kids over the years have been the ones who knew how to be funny and could comfortably engage the other kids around them. They weren't threatening or aloof or mocking; they were easygoing, and their sense of humor helped everyone around them feel more relaxed.

That's because humor does a lot of things, actually. It teaches our kids to be playful and lighthearted. It encourages them to be quick on their feet. It enables them to think multi-dimensionally and be critical thinkers. And it can ward off things like moodiness and depression. Not to mention that laughter, in general, is beneficial, because it actually oxygenates the blood and improves brain function. Oh, and it helps diffuse things like kid meltdowns. (Really hard for your sixth-grader to throw the remote at you if she's peeing herself laughing.)

In the same way that learning to play music or speak a foreign language or painting expands our children's learning capabilities, so, too, does humor and sarcasm. (Crazy, right?!) But it's like calisthenics for their brains. I mean, we encourage our kids to play sports as a form of exercise and learn an instrument to stimulate their neural processing, so doesn't it make perfect sense that we exercise their sense of humor too?

Humor is like calisthenics for our kids' brains.

Can We Hope for Funny Kids?

When Dave and I were first married, we were friends with this couple who had a six-year-old son. Super cute kid. He had a sense of humor like an edgy stand-up comic, and we loved that about him. He was funny but appropriate and everyone loved being around him.

Even at six, he got the essence of sarcasm. Chris was quick-witted and sharp, and we used to cross our fingers that when we had kids of our own, they'd have a sense of humor just like him. Having a kid with a good sense of humor is a gift. We agreed then that we were going to do our best work someday raising our kids to be able to hold their own on a sarcastic playing field. Over twenty years and two kids later, I'm happy to report that we've raised two exceptionally funny daughters (biased mother's opinion, of course). Both of our girls can hold their own in any sarcastic conversation. They know how to sling it, how to receive it, and how to temper it, both with their friends and with ours. And judging by how many comments we've gotten over the years about how funny our kids can be, I'm confident we've done right by them in helping them to enhance this part of their personality.

Since most new parents simply pray that their kids are well-behaved and stay under the radar in social situations, I realize that good sarcasm probably isn't on their top ten list of desired kid traits, but I think it should be. It really *is* okay to embrace having a kid with a sharp sense of humor. It's good for them and good for you because it's something you can bond over, believe it or not. We do with our girls. In fact, it's almost like a contest in our family to see who can be the most sarcastic. (Obviously different rules of sarcastic engagement apply to your immediate family and friends and the rest of the general population.)

Your family and friends will *get* you, while the rest of the world may or may not. Peoples' reaction to our sarcasm is a definite litmus test that helps us gauge which people are most like us and who we belong with for the long haul.

I vividly recall the first real conversation we had about the type of kids we hoped to have and how both of us wished that they'd be born with whatever magical DNA generates a healthy sense of sarcasm. You know, that certain gene that a person's born with that gives them perfect comedic timing. Well, we wanted that kid. And now there's absolutely nothing more gratifying than watching one of my daughters toss out a one-liner that has the ability to make people laugh—and think.

The reality is not everyone is wired to give or receive *or even understand* sarcastic humor. Just like not everyone is born with rhythm or the ability to do a split or hit a high note or pick up a guitar and just play. Like most things we learn, we can get comfortable with sarcasm with a little practice, some patience, and an open mind. When we encourage our kids to be spontaneous and playful and funny, it helps the juices flow a lot easier.

Teaching our kids the art of humor is almost like giving them another layer of skin that'll help insulate them against stress and tough times as they connect with the rest of the world.

Different Kinds of Humor

Remember, there are plenty of types of humor floating around out there and sarcasm is just one of them. There's improv, where people crack jokes on the fly; self-deprecating humor, which involves making fun of ourselves; slapstick that's mostly physical; dry humor that's matter-of-fact; and stand-up comedy that involves telling stories and jokes. Whatever kind of humor our kids gravitate to, it's our job to encourage them to develop their inner comedian. The more comfortable our kids get with being able to express their funny side, the better equipped they'll be to handle life's challenges.

> 📖 The younger a child is exposed to humor the more likely their sense of humor will emerge as a young adult. There are lots of benefits to developing skills around a good sense of humor, especially in the world we live in; we all could benefit from a good joke and a solid belly laugh.

When kids are young, though, they don't have a filter. That's a given. They hear stuff, they imitate it, and they get laughs and attention wherever and however they can. And that's not always a good thing. But, under the right conditions, the right kind of sarcasm can be cultivated and enhanced with guidance and support from loving sarcastic parents.

For instance, we need to teach our kids early on that it's not okay to walk up to someone they just met and say, "Hey, are you always this stupid or are you making an extra effort today?" That would be bad, not to mention insulting and off-putting and rude. But playfully criticizing my nieces when they were young and had trouble learning how to braid hair is different. Saying something like, "Wowwww, those braids look *amazing*" while I'm winking at them and starting the braid over from scratch is perfectly okay. That's because we already have a relationship and everyone understands how we're saying what we're saying. One of the most important things we should teach our kids is how to read the situational cues around them, like where they are, who they're with, and what kind of a relationship they have with the person on the receiving end. That way they don't embarrass themselves or someone else by hurling an insult when they meant to be funny.

We also need to help our kids understand that sarcasm has as much to do with what they're saying as how they're saying it. So that means we need to include a lesson about tone and inflection when we're helping them develop an appropriate sense of sarcasm. Here's what I mean: According to YourDictionary.com, *sarcasm sometimes depends on the tone of voice. These examples of sarcasm are replies to people or situations and would only be sarcastic with a sarcastic tone of voice:*

- When something bad happens—That's just what I need, great! Terrific.
- When you expected something to happen, especially after warning someone about it—Well what a surprise!
- When someone says something that is very obvious—Really Sherlock, no! You are clever.
- When someone does something wrong—Very good, well done, nice!
- When something happens that you don't want or need—That's just what we need![25]

📖 **A child's ability to apply humor and sarcasm effectively in a conversation might need some time to develop, like any other skill.**

At my house, Dave and I always try to take parenting in stride with a sarcastic, "Now I totally understand why animals eat their young." And whenever I remind our girls to straighten up their bedrooms when they're home on break, they pick up a stray bobby pin lying on the floor and say, "Okay, there you go. All good." Because, you know, college kids.

Remember, it's just as important to teach our kids how to handle sarcasm. If they are going to share it with family and friends, they have to understand how to receive it in the spirit that was intended. There may be times that feathers get ruffled or humor isn't received well. Learning how to roll with it can be another teachable moment. It is all about flexibility in the way we think.

Now don't get me wrong, I'm well aware that there is, and should be, a very distinct line between healthy, appropriately timed, harmless sarcasm and full-on snarkiness. That's why Dave and I raised our kids to know the difference. We both recognize that it's all too easy for people, especially kids, to cross the line and turn an innocent remark that's designed to be funny into something rude and chafing, which is definitely not okay.

We need to embrace and nurture all the beautiful qualities in our children, and this trait is no different. The trick is to coach our kids on where and when humor and sarcasm is applicable in their everyday lives. Start small, in the confines of the house. Take a few shots to the chin before you expose them to other people. Let them settle into a groove first and get a feel for what they can and can't say. Then, gradually, once they get their sea legs, let them loose on the rest of the world.

And if anyone judges you for having appropriately sarcastic kids, just tell them you're encouraging your kids to exercise their sarcastic side and they should be doing the same. (Just remember to say it in an ironic sounding tone.)

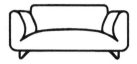

From the Couch of
Debra Fox Gansenberg MSW, LICSW

The younger a child is exposed to humor the more likely their sense of humor will emerge as a young adult. There are lots of benefits to developing skills around a good sense of humor, especially in the world we live in; we all could benefit from a good joke and a solid belly laugh.

Home life can get bogged down with all the things that have to get done and errands to run. Using humor at home can lighten the mood, 'cause unexpected smiles can make disciplining a little easier. A family who can laugh together will enjoy time together so much more.

Tip: In order to nurture a good sense of humor, you must create opportunities to make it happen. Participate in fun activities that will create laughter, like reading joke books and comics, playing safe practical jokes on each other, and watching funny movies together. Adopt a family tradition that includes a funny family *thing*. For example, everyone wears footie pajamas on Christmas morning or the same costume at Halloween. When you can share in a funny family experience together, chances are that a child's sense of humor will evolve and you will create wonderful funny memories together.

Tip: Like any skill building within the family, lead by example. If you want to hear laughter in the home, use laughter in the home. Tell an appropriate joke at the right time. Do a little teaching about timing and what would be an acceptable type of joke to tell depending on the audience. Kids are watching us—give them something fun to watch and learn.

Tip: When discipling our children, we need to ride a fine line between being firm, yet loving. Another way to lighten the mood during the parenting process is to keep the teachable moment lighthearted and use simple humor to try and communicate the lesson that needs to be taught and the rules that need to be followed.

A child's ability to apply humor and sarcasm effectively in a conversation might need some time to develop, like any other skill.

Tip: Have you ever created a fun time and your kids take it one step too far? Kids have a knack for not knowing when enough is enough. It is our job as adults to teach how to use humor or sarcasm if we are using it in the home. Kids don't always know when it's a good time to tell a joke or what might be off-color or inappropriate, so take the time to explain these important details, use a teachable moment.

Tip: Some practical and fun ways to use humor in the home might include altering your voice to something funny like a barking dog, fake crying like you are really upset by something he/she said, or pretending you can't hear your child—especially when he is whining. Once your kids see you do these things they will most likely begin to try and build these same skills, which could be rather entertaining.

Tip: Our kids are often exposed to sarcasm and humor through television, YouTube videos, and books. When you are watching or witnessing others being sarcastic or funny name it, and help them identify these various ways of communicating. Have them practice by telling a few jokes or trying reasonable sarcastic remarks.

Message: Using sarcasm and humor can be a complicated subject. When it is used, you need to be very careful about how it is interpreted because feelings can get hurt. The fact of the matter is, the more you are around humor and sarcasm, the more you understand how to use both appropriately. Create space for your child to let you know how he feels or what he thinks when a joke or sarcasm can be confusing. Sometimes what one person might think is funny, another person might not. Explaining this to your child is helpful whether he is telling the joke or is on the receiving end of it.

Survival Tip 16:

Technology Is a Part of Everyone's Life Now, So Get Used to It

We need to teach our kids that there's a time and a place for technology.

Back in the day, when we were all kids, we entertained ourselves rather differently than our kids entertain themselves today. When we were young, we had stuff like markers and colored paper and skateboards and VHS tapes. We played HORSE and hide-and-seek. We played Barbie and GI Joe. We actually played catch and climbed trees (in some cases falling out of them). And with the exception of maybe an Atari 2600 that some kid got for his Bar Mitzvah, most everything else we did involved some level of creativity and hands-on play. Short of abusing their TV privileges a little, kids didn't spend all their time staring at screens the way they do now. Life was simpler in a lot of ways, but, as civilizations do, we evolved. And our kids evolved right along with it. We're now responsible for setting limits on technology and screen time and encouraging our kids to spend some time just being kids.

Today's youth live in an entirely different world. They're inundated with iPads and iPhones and Xboxes and tablets and touch screens and gaming systems that fit in their back pocket. They're clicking and dragging and swiping their brains out. And they have an endless array of super-slick equipment to choose from to occupy their time. The most obvious downside is that all these options are keeping them from all the old-fashioned ways of spending their free time. (Not to mention cutting in to all the time they could be spending with us.)

Though all this technology represents a different kind of fun factor to our kids, unrivaled by anything we had growing up, the reality is that it's taking them away from the pickup games and the bike rides and the afternoons running around playing Manhunt in the neighborhood. Now, with technology being so accessible, our kids have the ability, even at a really young age, to engross themselves in games and media that can stream forever. Like, for-ever. And that's something we can't relate to because we didn't grow up in a digital world. The most we could do was sit in front of the TV all day and night until the station stopped broadcasting at midnight. (Big night!) Otherwise, we could get lost in books (*if* we were readers). Beyond that, we had to *find* things to do. We had to get creative.

Technology 24/7

Our kids don't have to get creative in the same ways we did. All the activities they want are in an app or on a website, just a quick click away. The thinking is gone. And since the content is never-ending, it's like they've got a built-in buddy and babysitter 24/7. They've got constant companionship and entertainment without ever having to leave their room.

The fact is, we're vying pretty heavily for our kid's attention in ways that our parents never had to because the gravitational pull of all this technology is more or less irresistible to today's kids, and they're being exposed to all these electronics earlier and earlier. They're getting immersed in technology almost as soon as they can walk and talk. This presents a big problem for us, because it's all they know.

They can go anywhere, entertain themselves twenty-four hours a day, and, theoretically, never leave the couch while they're doing it. All with pocket-size devices that fit perfectly in their hot little hands. The downside to that is that they're not using their bodies to physically go *anywhere*. With all the glitzy, engaging gadgets all around them, our kids are being lured away from traditional kinds of entertainment, like getting out and exercising and using their own imagination. They're spending less and less time talking to each other face-to-face or even in real time voice-to-voice over the phone and more and more time secluded and staring down at some kind of a screen. They're joining online gaming communities and playing virtually, instead of getting outside and running around and getting sweaty and using their bodies and creative minds. And that's not good.

So the big question on every parent's mind is: *Is technology wrecking our kids?* Is all this screen time damaging them intellectually and emotionally and physically and stunting their growth and frying their brains? Not easy questions to answer, because the answer really depends almost exclusively on how we handle the amount of time they spend on all their devices.

> 📖 **When was the last time your entire family had a tech-free day? Try it. You might actually have fun. It might seem impossible, but in different parts of the world, unplugging is done all the time.**

If we let our kids lock themselves in their bedroom and be digital all day, like a lot of young kids would love to do, then, in addition to being severely vitamin D deficient, our kids will have zero muscle tone, no interpersonal communication skills, and no endurance whatsoever. They'll basically be lonely, isolated, little hermits with really, really pale skin.

When my kids were young and they had their first cell phones, I felt an immeasurable sense of relief that I could reach out and connect with them any time I needed them and vice versa. As a mom, it was like having the world's longest umbilical cord attached to both of my kids. I always had the ability to reach out to them, unless, of course, one of them was being snarky and turned off their location services. (Oh yeah, that happened.) There's an incredible comfort level that comes with being able to stay connected. That's the true upside with all this technology.

Keep in mind, my girls grew up just on the cusp of the social media explosion—stuff like Facebook and Twitter were barely emerging when they were young. (Thank God.) All they had were basic multi-player online games like Club Penguin and Webkinz, little virtual worlds where they could goof around with other kids in a cutesy little cyber world filled with limited chat capabilities and comic strip characters. (Not a lot to worry about in Webkinz World.) In spite of the fact that most age-appropriate games available at that time were pretty rudimentary, my oldest daughter still managed to lose a few shades of skin pigment hanging out in her room playing those games. It wasn't until we saw how affected she was by direct sunlight when we opened her curtains in the middle of the day, that we realized she was a little too consumed. Suffice it to say, we pulled the plug and threw her outside in the backyard and made her climb some trees and breathe in some fresh air. Within a short time, she was able to see how much she was missing by being indoors on her computer for hours at a time.

That's the fundamental problem with technology: knowing when enough is enough. And since each kid is so different, those limits vary from household to household. Some kids have the natural ability to self-regulate better than others. Those who are just more attracted to technology are the ones who need a little extra kick in the pants to unplug.

As far as cell phones were concerned, they both got basic flip phones when they hit the fourth grade around age nine. They didn't have texting, and they didn't have internet capabilities. All they had was the ability to send and receive calls. That's it. And that was true of most of their little friends.

Now, though, even just a handful of years later, so much has changed. Today kids are using cellphones at an even earlier age. Gone are the days of little kids getting base-model cell phones just to be able to check in with Mommy and Daddy after school. That's been replaced by grammar school kids walking around with the newest generation iPhone that's been pimped out with unlimited data and texting. I'd see eight-, nine-, ten-year-old kids walking past me in the pickup line wearing a two-hundred-dollar pair of Beats headphones and carrying a newer, more powerful cellphone than I had in my purse.

That's how much and how fast times are changing. According to a 2017 resource guide for parents by Jacqueline Howard on CNN. com, "about 45 percent of US children age ten to twelve had their own smartphone with a service plan."[26] Ten to twelve years old! Even though that sounds ridiculously young, it's becoming more and more mainstream to see little kids walking around with phablets bigger than their own heads. They all have them. Don't forget: if we're noticing what they have, you can bet that your kids are noticing who has what too. Therein lies the problem.

Remember, our kids are the first real generation to grow up in the Digital Age. That means that they've grown up in a digital world where everyone's connected and there's a cell phone in every back pocket. That's just the world we're living in. The world *they're* living in.

Gen Z Has a Different Communication Style

It's up to us to help them learn to balance time on electronics with time on everything else. Because as our kids get older, they're faced with a very different kind of addiction than we had growing up. They're battling the constant temptation of devices and screens and social media in ways that most of us can't even understand. In-your-hands technology didn't exist when we were kids.

The choices we had for things to occupy our time twenty or thirty years ago could be equated to shopping at the Gap versus shopping at Macy's—we just didn't have as many options, but we were always entertained in spite of the limited choices we had. Ignorance was bliss, I guess.

As the parents of the first kids to be raised in a totally technology-driven world, we're in uncharted territory. We're pioneers raising the first generation of totally tech-savvy kids. And most of us are making up the rules as we go along. Not to mention trying to keep up with the technology learning curve. We have to know what our kids are doing online and on their phones, and we've got to be able to understand it ourselves. That can be pretty intimidating for young parents. Which is exactly why we can't stress out too much about our kids being connected and being online. It's part of their culture—part of the world they're growing up in.

We have to remind ourselves every day that our kids never grew up talking on the phone to their friends like we did. Sad as it is, today's digital generation is interacting with each other in very different ways. Perfect example: my girls literally laugh at me when I suggest that they pick up the phone and call their friends. *No one calls anyone, Mom*, they'll both say. And it's true, they don't. Instead, they Snapchat and post and tweet and tag. It's different. Very, very different. They've got computers in every classroom; they're doing schoolwork on their phones; they're using devices in school every day. This is the new world. There's little or no opportunity for our kids to get away from technology. Now that kids are on tablets and laptops in school, technology follows them everywhere. In fact, according to a 2017 *New York Times* article by Natasha Singer, "more than half the nation's primary- and secondary school students—more than 30 million children—use Google education apps, the company says."[27] That's a huge number.

I'm a Believer in Limits!

Now look, I'm a supporter of all the technology around us because it's definitely got its obvious benefits. Above all, it allows us all to stay connected—a super-critical factor for parents wanting to keep tabs on our kids. Technology also gives our kids unlimited platforms to explore their creativity. Whether they're into art or music or design or photography or anything else they can think of, they have an entire world of resources sitting only a click away. But I'm also a big believer in limits, because limits are the key to ensuring that our kids keep their priorities straight from an early age. Everything in moderation, right?

In our house, we had a no-devices-at-the-dinner-table rule that we still have today. Dave and I modeled it straight from the top. No one, including us, was allowed to pull out a phone or a Nintendo DS at the kitchen table, in a restaurant, or at a friend's house, and that was just the rule. Period. Still is. Believe me, my kids notice who does and who doesn't whenever we go out. They also know never to *dare* have a conversation with me while looking at a screen. They wouldn't dream of it. It's just rude. We consider it a courtesy thing, something that's non-negotiable.

Unfortunately, we can only fight the fight so far, because the reality is that we live in a digital world where our kids are being expected to use technology at school and at work and as a means of staying connected. It's just how our society has evolved. Still, we have the ability as parents to mandate certain rules, in spite of what other people are doing around us. It's our job to set limits with our kids and ensure they grow up knowing that technology has a very specific place and role in our world. In other words, we absolutely have to be willing to take that phone or controller out of their hands if they're not toeing the line. That's how we make it work. That's how we help them understand.

It's our job to set limits with our kids and ensure they grow up knowing that technology has a very specific place.

So how young is too young for all of this technology? Well, that's a tough one because kids are seeming more mature and savvier at younger and younger ages nowadays. But there is research out there suggesting that too much at a young age is detrimental. In her 2018 *Verywell Family* article, "The Harmful Effects of Too Much Screen Time for Kids," Amy Morin says that too much screen time for young kids causes everything from obesity and sleep problems to behavior and educational issues and even violence.[28]

Look, with my kids, social media wasn't quite mainstream when they were young. We had *that* going for us. But the world is changing so quickly. Just five years ago, kids started getting iPhones, even in the lower grades like third and fourth. That all changed in June of 2007 when Apple released the first iPhone. Now, learning all the new apps and interfaces is like learning Latin from scratch in a weekend (at least for the parents).

Remember, the potential for addiction with these things is always there, just under the surface, which is why we have to stay on top of what they're doing and how long they're doing it. We have to assert our authority and our ability to take all this stuff away in a blink. Because without any expectations or limit setting, most kids just don't have the capacity to self-regulate.

> 📖 **Too much of anything isn't a good thing. How do you know when too much technology is a problem? Anything that disrupts the quality of one's life on a daily basis is worth a look at.**

Even in our family, where Dave has worked for Microsoft for over a decade and we were always surrounded by the newest, hottest technology, we knew how important limits were for our girls. We knew that a virtual world, no matter how enticing and exciting, could never replace the real world. So we insisted that our kids get on Razor scooters and bikes and swing sets and climb trees and hike and leave their devices behind.

A virtual world, no matter how enticing and exciting, could never replace the real world.

We make rules and we enforce them. We teach our kids, at an early age, not to be dependent on devices. We teach them to look up, often, so they don't miss the world around them. We make sure they know how to pick up all the social and emotional cues around them, even though they have technology in their hands. We remind them that texting us or their friends from the other room is *not* okay. (Unless, of course, you need them to turn down the TV, and you're all comfy in the bedroom and they're in the living room. In that case it's totally fine.)

I actually had a parent come to me, when my girls were in grammar school, complaining that she couldn't get her own girls to break away from their phones. She whined and moaned to me about how constantly distracted they were and had no idea whatsoever how to manage their overindulgence. To which I reminded her (sans the dope slap that I really wanted to give her) that *she* was the parent. *She* was the one who made the rules and bought the phones and *she* paid for the cell service. I think it was a defining moment for her, because I openly called her out on dropping the ball as a parent. I reminded her that how her kids used or abused the technology *she* gave them, was on her.

Let me say again: it's up to us and us alone to prevent technology from ruining our kids. In spite of how challenging it might look to maintain a healthy balance with all this stuff in their lives, it's really not all that hard. We just have to **hold the line**, no matter what. We carve out family time and time for books and time for creativity and time for exercise—and technology just becomes another little thing that we fit into our day-to-day world. It fits in the way *we* show them it fits in. We make the rules. And if they're not okay with that (because they *will* push back, them being kids and all), then we pull the plug and hand them a bunch of rocks to play with. They'll get with the program eventually.

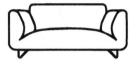

From the Couch of
Debra Fox Gansenberg MSW, LICSW

When was the last time your entire family had a tech-free day? Try it. You might actually have fun. It might seem impossible, but in different parts of the world, unplugging is done all the time.

Tip: Before you request disconnecting, plan ahead and create some family time that stimulates interaction that creates opportunity for fun and connection. If it is simply scheduled into your daily routine it won't feel so awful.

Tip: Eat your meals with NO phones or TVs allowed! Remind everyone that this is a time to talk about your day and plan ahead for the next. This will cut down on kids socializing during dinner, as well as enable parents to focus their attention on their children. Remember how dinner conversation was actually fun and rather useful to learn what is going on in everyone's lives?

Tip: Save play time on screens for a family activity; doing it together will create common conversations and interactive play. Start a tournament or request a challenge against another family member. Now this could be fun!

Tip: Find a home for all of the electronics in the family. Create a designated spot where they sleep, rest, charge, and live when not being used. Lock them up if you have to—to keep them safe from any desperate little hands.

Message: As adults who lived a life before screens and technology, we remember the good ol' days. As a society, we learn a lot from having access to so much technology, but there is a time and a place to learn and explore. Nurturing tech-free activity in the home is a healthy alternative to always being engaged with devices. Teach your kids what the ol' days looked like by re-living them together.

Too much of anything isn't a good thing. How do you know when too much technology is a problem? Anything that disrupts the quality of one's life on a daily basis is worth a look at.

Gen Zers are having a hard time staying entertained and in need of a lot of stimulation and activity as a result of an increase in use of technology. Having a hard time sitting still is also a concern for many children of this generation, so don't look the other way when it comes to screen time. You are the leader of the pack; set the tone. Watch your own use and model the behavior you're expecting from your own child.

Tip: Just recently devices are equipped with the statistics of each individual's personal use of device. Familiarize yourself with the "Screen Time" box located somewhere on your child's device. There are now apps and systems in place to manage and control how much time can be spent on specific apps, sites, or parts of the device. Go confidently to your child and set your rules and limits, state your expectations, and remind then who is in control.

Tip: A common discussion amongst parents of Gen Zers is when the right age is to allow technology into your child's life. This decision is clearly yours, Mom and Dad, but there are pros and cons to consider. Anything before eighteen months is using technology for *your* benefit, not your child's. They are only asking for it if they are taught it is something for them. The best rule of thumb is to put it off until there is an actual benefit to your child's use. Between eighteen to twenty-four months, exposure to educational apps and programs are fine for your toddler with your assistance. Watching along is a great way to enhance their learning experience and have interactive play time together.

Tip: Before introducing screens to your kids, take time to look at the warning signs of addiction to screens. You may not think it could happen to you or your kids, but screen addiction is occurring more often than ever due to increased use in homes and schools.

- If you give your child a limit or stop time and they repeatedly go over their allotment or totally disregard or lose track of time this could be a red flag.
- If you ask your child when the last time he spent time with his friends was and he/she considers contact by screens as socializing,

then screens most definitely could be interfering with his/her social life and ability to interact with people in real time. If your child has difficulty socializing and interacting with family or friends without a device, this too could be a sign that a serious problem is developing.

- If screens are a constant bone of contention and result in fighting and/or behavior problems and cannot be put away with ease, this is a sign that things need to change. Children who struggle with an addiction to their screens might show signs of withdrawal when asked to put their phone or iPad away. If you frequently witness your child become irritable, easily frustrated, withdrawn, or depressed when asked to separate from their screen, this could be a red flag.
- Have you ever caught your child sneaking his phone or iPad when his time is over and it is put away for the night or lost as a punishment? Lying about their use and needing more time because he/she just can't seem to get enough are both behaviors to look at more seriously.

Your child might not be an addict . . . yet, so take precautions and understand what to look for to know when it is a problem. When it comes to screens, it is important not to just look at how much time a child is on their devices, but also how they use their time as well. Look at the use of technology in the home to learn the habits forming in the household. It might be necessary to adjust your family habits.

Survival Tip 17:

Remind Your Kid That Everything Doesn't Belong to Them

The sooner you get your kids comfortable with sharing the better.

Sometimes we have to share. We just do. Not because we necessarily want to (like giving up the really big flowers on the delish-looking slice of birthday cake) or even because we should (like giving up our seat to the pregnant lady on the train), but simply because it's what people need to do to get along. Unfortunately, though, not everyone does it well, and teaching it to our kids can be super stressful. But it's a way more important life skill than most of us realize—a critical skill that our kids have to learn, whether they want to or not.

Now the average person can usually suck it up and share, even if it isn't our first choice. We're adults, so most of us have learned the importance and the necessity of sharing. We get that it's just an obligatory people skill. Toss a couple of young, immature kids into the mix who are both after the same basketball or Hula-Hoop, and all bets are off. Then it's a complete free-for-all. That's because learning to part with things, especially things we like or enjoy, isn't easy. And it's especially challenging for kids.

Like we do with every other life skill our kids have to learn, we hammer at them to get comfortable with sharing because it's something they're going to have to be able to do throughout their life. And we start early, because there's always the potential for hair-pulling or shoving or meltdowns when you put kids together in any given situation. It's just natural that potential explodes when one of them wants what the other one has. So the sooner we teach them that sharing is just a necessary part of life, the better.

Of course, we all expect toddlers to be awful at parting with stuff because toddlers are egocentric, selfish little people. It's a fact. Any of us who've ever had a toddler know it. But the expectation is that, eventually, our greedy little guys who hate to hand stuff over will evolve into generous, mature kindergarteners and adolescents who are happy to share. The problem is, that doesn't always happen quite as soon or quite as easily as we'd all like. The reason is that, to little kids, the word *sharing* and the concept behind it is meaningless. They don't see any good reason why they need to give up their dolls or their toys or give their friend a turn on the swing—at least not right away.

> 🛋 **Did you ever have something that was so invaluable to you that sharing it was out of the question? For really young children, that experience includes just about everything they own—their blankie, stuffed animal, juice cup, or socks. Sharing is caring; take the time to show them how.**

Squish Away

I mean sure, our kids do ultimately learn that they have to share or let other people have a chance using their stuff, but it certainly doesn't happen overnight even though we desperately wish it would. Sharing is very much a learned skill. It's one of those abilities that needs to be taught and reinforced and retaught and re-reinforced for what seems like forever. This is why we have to be tireless in our efforts to drill the concept into their heads.

Now technically speaking, kids don't even have a shot at grasping the concept of sharing until they're around five. Coincidentally, this is about the time they start school and begin interacting regularly with other non-sharers. (Great timing.) Not to worry, though, kids are pretty moldable as a general rule. A lot like Play-Doh, I've found. We just have to keep squishing them into the shape we want and, eventually, they harden that way.

We also have to get creative when we're teaching our kids these skills. Kind of like how we have to get creative when we sneak veggies into our kid's lunches. You know, how we grind them up so they're unrecognizable and then camouflage them as other things so our kids can't detect them. The same goes with sharing.

We can make a game out of it so they don't realize we're actually teaching them a valuable life skill. Try keeping a tally of how many doors they hold open for people or how many times they say *please* and *thank you* or how often they clear the dishes at home or how many times they share their toys during a playdate. Then we celebrate those moments with a little praise and recognition and maybe a Blow Pop, just like we do when they swallow down a big forkful of spinach. Because it's good for them, and we want them to remember.

Make sharing a game so they don't realize we're actually teaching them a valuable life skill.

Unfortunately, though, not everybody has the aptitude for sharing. There are plenty of people—kids and grown-ups—who just can't do it, no matter how much they're taught that they should. As a mom, seeing those types of people only strengthens my resolve to ensure that I get the point across with my own kids. And it should do the same for you.

Seeing kids struggle with sharing is pretty common and expected. It's just one part of the learning process. But we've all seen those adults who completely lack the capacity to share. Those people drive me nuts. Those are the people I just want to grab by the shoulders and shake vigorously until they get it. (But since I'm a lover, not a fighter, I don't.) We've all felt it when we see people like the guy at the mall who whizzes into the parking spot you've been patiently idling in front of for five minutes, or the friends who refuse to compromise on where you go out to eat, or the woman at the office who constantly talks about herself, or the husband who won't share the remote (not you, Dave, don't worry). It's a real disappointment when you see that kind of behavior from an adult.

But we more or less expect it from kids because kids are naturally territorial. They also get easily attached to stuff, which makes it even tougher for them to learn how to play cooperatively. Because they're convinced that having their friend's Luke Skywalker action figure is the *only* thing on the planet that will make them happy. That, and they completely lack the ability when they're young to part with anything. But we're the adults, so modeling good behavior is entirely up to us. We need to get it right—for our kid's sake.

> 🛋 It is true that our children at all stages of development are watching us. Their observations shape their decision making and judgement and ultimately their behavior. Parents, we need to teach our kids through our modeling, so watch your own behavior.

Modeling good behavior is entirely up to us.

When my girls were young, like super-impressionable kindergarten-age, I used to purposely let Dave have the remote once in a while when we were watching TV with the girls. Now make no mistake, I really didn't want to give up watching the Food Network, but I did it anyway as a carefully orchestrated parenting move to model good behavior for my kids. I did stuff like that all the time. Like I'd be savagely craving Italian for dinner, but I'd still openly ask everyone in my family where *they* wanted to eat. Or I'd almost always give my girls free rein over the music they listened to in the car, painful as that was (there's only so much *Top 40 Countdown* a human being can take). It was the easy, relatively small stuff like that that helped subtly reinforce the fact that Dave and I knew how to share too. While that didn't keep my kids from screwing up and not sharing sometimes, I think it definitely helped strengthen my argument that everyone needs to be able to do it. And since Dave and I were walking the walk ourselves every chance we got, the behavior came straight from the top down.

But no parenting technique is foolproof, and my kids tended to forget certain rules of engagement at least as often as they would remember them. The sharing rule was a biggie for forgetting. This is why so many interactions between my girls would predictably end up in one of them crying or whining because the other one couldn't let her lie on the living room couch to watch TV, or they couldn't give their sister a turn sitting in the front seat of the car, or one of them was hogging all the beach toys. It's unavoidable. But that's just the road we have to follow when we have kids. We have to absorb the bumps and chunks of broken asphalt until the road smooths out a little and the ride becomes a little smoother. Thankfully it does. It just takes about ninety-thousand miles worth of travel to get there.

See, sharing is just another one of those ethical, moral lessons kids need a while to learn and digest. And since I'm not about blowing sunshine, I'm being honest that it's a constant challenge. We're always sharing stuff, to varying degrees—stuff like our space or our time or our friends or our opinions—so we have to get adept at being able to do it or we're setting ourselves up for a rough ride. Most of us plan on inter-acting with other people throughout our lifetime. And the sooner we get our kids comfortable with that idea, the better off everyone will be.

So how do we help? How do we handle it when our kid won't hand over the Barbie or share the bowl of grapes or give another kid a turn at bat? Well, we do exactly what we do when we teach them any life skill—we clarify why it's important and then we set the expectation. We don't ever force them to share, because kids inherently reject any-thing we force them to do. So instead, we make sharing appealing by promoting its benefits, like how good it will make them or the people they're sharing with feel. More than that, if they share, it'll motivate other kids to share with them as well. We encourage them to do it every chance we get. We guide them in knowing when it's appropriate to share and when they really don't have to. That's how we make it happen.

We use tricks like timers that divide up the time fairly, and if our kids just can't get there on their own, then we time-out the thing that they can't part with. Don't time-out the kid, just remove the thing that they're having trouble giving up from the equation. Then we explain that until everyone can learn how to take turns, it's off limits. We keep it all positive. We model *all* of that ourselves and we make sure our kids see us doing it. We make that modeling into teachable moments.

Make Your Home a Sharing Haven

The truth is, having something that someone else wants is a powerful position to be in, and kids pick up on that pretty early on in their lives.

That's why we have to cultivate an environment where our kids are used to and comfortable with sharing. Because if our daughter can't let Suzie have a turn with her American Girl doll in the second grade, then she's not going to learn how to work or live or collaborate with other people later on in life. That's just the harsh truth.

Look, in the beginning, letting people use our stuff or have what we want is painful. I mean, it's painful at times even when we're adults. But letting someone have a turn with something doesn't mean we're losing it forever. It's not a permanent giveaway. It's usually a back and forth—at least in theory. Sharing means that you, too, will soon have a turn. This is the key factor that we always have to stress with our kids. Over and over and over.

Show your kids that sharing means that they, too, will soon have a turn.

At the same time (and I know this sounds kind of counterintuitive) kids shouldn't be expected to share *everything*. It's actually okay for certain, special things to be reserved just for them. Although if my girls had their way, every single solitary possession they had growing up would fall under that category just as a loophole. In all fairness, it really is a good thing to have a handful of special toys or dolls or pieces of clothing that are ours and ours alone. I believe this because it's a respect thing. It's important to recognize that even if we live in a family environment where things are regularly borrowed and shared, we're allowed to preserve a little bit of ownership over a few special things. It's called having boundaries and, to a degree, that's okay—especially with siblings. Because even if most things are communal, not everything needs to be. Everyone deserves to have a little individuality and personal space.

What If There Is No One around to Share With

For those of you raising an only child, though, I know you're especially worried right now about whether your kid will grow up knowing how to share. Because without another child to have to learn to share with, it's natural to wonder how an only child will learn to interact when other kids are thrown into the mix. I know this because I was that only child. I was the kid who grew up having carte blanche over everything in my house because there was no competition.

> 📖 **When you are the only child in a family and learn to share and communicate with mature adults, interacting with other children your age can be difficult.**

I've had plenty of conversations over the years with my mom about how she was consciously aware of the potential for me to grow up into a spoiled little brat. Because, let's be honest, only children do, by default, have that reputation. Most people hear *only child* and they automatically think of qualities like overindulged, self-centered, and obnoxious. Trust me, over the course of my lifetime, I've had countless people tell me how shocked they were to find out that I was an only child. They were surprised because I just never behaved like the stereotypical only child. I was always really comfortable sharing; I was always very sensitive of other people's feelings; I thrived on being a team player. That's how I was raised.

Even though I didn't have to jockey for my mom or dad's attention growing up or fight with a brother for the remote or lend a sister my favorite hoodie, I still learned, very early on, that it wasn't all about me. My parents taught me to always consider the people around me and act accordingly, because we live in a big world where everybody has to get along and no one cares if you were raised with or without siblings. All people care about is that you know how to behave like a rational, kind, considerate human being.

As far as I'm concerned, traits like thoughtfulness aren't genetic. Being considerate of others is something we learn. And we learn it from the top down. Parents set the tone at home. In every home. We set it every step of the way. I don't care where someone grew up or what they have or don't have. The kind of predisposition a kid has is a direct result of the environment *we* create.

So if we raise a kid with an elitist or entitled or snotty attitude who doesn't know how to share and be considerate of other people, then we should naturally assume that our kids learned that from somewhere. Duh. At that point, we should be looking squarely in the mirror, 'cause that's where it's coming from.

If we don't stress that our kids have to take turns, then they'll never pass the ball. If we don't stress that our kids have to be kind, then they'll be little snots around everyone else. If we don't stress that our kids need to include everyone, then they'll be snobs. It's that simple.

I can't even put an accurate number on how many entitled kids I've seen come through my school over the years. But I *can* tell you from personal interactions with them and their parents that they're little carbon copies of their moms and dads—rude and self-absorbed and bossy. They're the kids who demanded all the new crayons in art class or threw a fit when they struck out at whiffle ball or when they couldn't sit next to their best friend at lunch. I had kids who were so bad at sharing that they literally couldn't handle it when other kids got to read out loud in class and they didn't. Selfishness takes on many forms.

That's why it's so critical that we teach our kids to be considerate and empathetic since there are *always* going to be other people who want and need the same things they do—maybe even at the exact same second that we need it. By teaching our kids to give up pole position in the sandbox just because someone else might like that spot, we're actually helping them cultivate a spirit of generosity. And that can carry a person a long, long way in their lifetime.

In the spirit of setting a strong example for our kids, we have to make a steady, concerted effort to hand over the clicker or share the car radio or divvy up the chores around the house, because whether we realize it or not, our kids are watching. They're watching everything we do and listening to everything we say, and they're imitating. Heavily. And since we're the ones they look to first as role models for good behavior, we have to be on point with this stuff all the time. Like 24/7. Solid kid sharers come from one place . . . great parent sharers.

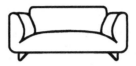

From the Couch of
Debra Fox Gansenberg MSW, LICSW

Did you ever have something that was so invaluable to you that sharing it was out of the question? For really young children that experience includes just about everything they own their blankie, stuffed animal, juice cup, or socks. Sharing is caring; take the time to show them how.

Tip: When teaching a dog a new trick we use treats to reinforce the new behavior; how about doing the same thing for our children? Positive reinforcement encourages interest, motivation, and ultimately the new behavior. If Sammy has a new blanket and doesn't want to share it with his little brother, how about offering some incentive to change the outcome: "If you can share just a corner of your blankie with Teddy, then you may have ten extra minutes to watch television." Using if/then situations is a great way to show kids they have a chance to change their behavior/outcome.

Tip: Whether your child is five or fifteen, if he/she is not ready to share a certain personal belonging, if time allows, give your child a space to put their item off limits to sharing temporarily. This allows the child to feel like they have a say and that can reduce their anxiety or discomfort about sharing. This way, when they are ready to share, they can do it on their own terms, which increases the chances of sharing in the future.

Tip: Oftentimes when we think of sharing, we think of physical things. However, sometimes sharing might include someone's help, someone's time, or even a special story. When a household is busy or filled with multiple kids and tasks to be accomplished, lending a helping hand is a great way of sharing your time or assistance. One way to encourage sharing in this way could include a great if/then scenario. "Matthew, if you can share the big comfy chair with me then I can share my time with both you and Ryan for a story, because we all can fit," or "Joey, if you share that funny story you know about the purple cat, then I think it might make your little sister smile."

Message: Like any skill, sharing is one that can take some children a little more time to develop than others. Create opportunities in the home to practice asking for someone to share, as well as offering to share with others. This way kids will learn that sharing is a two-way street.

It is true that our children at all stages of development are watching us. Their observations shape their decision making and judgement and ultimately their behavior. Parents, we need to teach our kids through our modeling, so watch your own behavior.

Do you remember a person in your life growing up that you really wanted to be like? Did you want to wear a jean jacket like your babysitter or have long hair like your guitar teacher? Do your kids want to be just like you—singing just like Mommy or shaving just like Daddy? Kids don't need to be just like their parents but they can *act* just like us!

Tip: Learning by observing is a common way individuals process information. Young children do most of their learning by watching and listening to things around them, and this practice continues throughout their lifetime. As parents, we must consider that we are often the source of a lot of their information just by living and sharing space with our kids 24/7. Take an inventory of your behavior: Is it good, unhealthy, or respectful? We are human, no one is perfect; however, it is important to check in to see if our behavior is really acceptable. A good rule of thumb to practice: If you saw your child do what you just did or said, would you be okay with that? Remember, we are influential because we are Mom and Dad.

Tip: Friends and family also influence our children through their behavior. Kids spend a lot of time with other kids, and hopefully with extended family members as well. If you see a family member doing something that makes you uncomfortable or has your child behaving in a way that is not okay with you, teach your family members about your expectations. Your kids' friends also shape their behavior. If a friend goes around swearing or name-calling and your child thinks it's funny, there is a chance he will try it out himself. Address the behavior with both of them if you were present at the time or, if not, address this with your child after the playdate is over. As kids get older, this issue becomes more complex because the behaviors can be complicated and a bit riskier. If you suspect that your child might be engaging in a risky behavior, encourage them to stop and think about the impact of their choices and weigh the consequences of the behavior. Then encourage them to make the choice that makes the most sense for *them*, not their friends or peers.

Tip: The good news about modeling good behavior is that you can teach your kids wonderful things like sewing, building models, fishing, or knitting. Take your time and make a list with your children of all the skills they would like to know how to do. The skills that can be taught are endless, and if you can't do it, enlist help.

Message: Parents might say they have eyes on the back of their head and are always watching, but most kids have three sets of ears. They are always listening! Be mindful of your actions and words because we have the responsibility to teach our children incredible things through our own behavior. When it comes to swearing, smoking, or slamming a door, they can see those things too. If your child has witnessed something you are less than proud of, loop back around and take the time to own it, name it as not okay, and apologize if necessary. By addressing a not-so-good behavior, you are teaching your kids you are not perfect and when you make a mistake, you will own it. Now that's a great behavior to model!

When you are the only child in a family and learn to share and communicate with mature adults, interacting with other children your age can be difficult.

A common dilemma for families with only one child is the important task of teaching social skills so your child can assimilate successfully into peer groups. Parents need to get creative creating opportunities for their only kids to interact and learn how to engage well with other children.

Tip: An important detail when it comes to parenting a single child is not to force anything too quickly or too soon. These kids are often forced to share at playdates or parties without much practice. Role play with stuffed animals or make-believe friends to act out possible scenarios that he/she might encounter. If a child is given the chance to back up and work at his/her own pace and have a chance to feel prepared, it will increase his chances of sharing or interacting in the near future.

Tip: Make sure your only child doesn't run the show. Implementing and enforcing rules is important; this will prevent a selfish or badly-behaved, bossy only child. Sometimes parents simply forget that there needs to be a "no" or a "have to" at times when it comes to parenting your only child.

Tip: One sure way your only child will have to share is to have other kids around. Make it a priority to include your child's friends in simple play dates, road trips, or activities. When others are present, use teachable moments to model sharing, consideration for the other's needs, and good listening.

Tip: Encourage your only child to get involved in school activities or local team sports. There is no "I" in team, so your child will quickly learn that his performance is not just about the end result, but rather the team's outcome. When playing lacrosse, learning to pass the ball and share in the process of scoring a goal is the important lesson. "AJ, you didn't win your lacrosse game all by yourself; your team won. Congratulations!"

In order to avoid a selfish ill-mannered only child, create opportunities to connect. Host a social event, take a friend on a trip, or get them involved with a club so that your only child can practice skills as often as he/she can. In time, your only child will welcome others, share well, communicate successfully, and behave appropriately when spending time with other children. Celebrate their successes by complimenting them when you see them doing well. Your child will grow in ability to share and in self-confidence.

Just Keep Talking the Talk; Eventually They'll Be Walking the Walk

In the end, our kids do learn to listen to us, and we learn to listen too.

Is anyone listening to me? Because I know words are coming out of my mouth. I can hear them. And so can everyone else around us . . . except you. Come on!

I think this pretty much sums up how most of us feel when we try to communicate with our kids—at least the majority of the time. We parents do all the talking, we make all the requests, we toss out all the directions, and our kids selectively pick and choose which things they want to respond to—and when. It's called **selective hearing**. And it's real. Very, very real.

While this selective hearing condition doesn't really fully kick in until our kids are in middle school, it most definitely shows itself once our kids start feeling a little independent—like once they start heading off to school. As they realize they're old enough to be out on their own a little (even if that just means being in a supervised classroom for a few hours a day), they fancy themselves ready to take on the world. Almost instinctively, they start thinking they don't need to hear what we have to say anymore. That becomes a bit of a problem when we're the ones trying to teach them everything they need to know to survive in this world.

Cricket! Cricket!

Ever hear the expression "falling on deaf ears"? Well, after raising two kids, I can definitively say that there's no doubt in my mind that that phrase was coined by a frustrated parent. Probably some mom who'd been yelling at her son through the kitchen window to come inside for dinner while the kid played on—in spite of the fact that he was looking directly at her while she was yelling to him.

See, once our kids figure out that they can *pretend* to ignore us, they gain a little bit of an upper hand. At least they think they do. At any given time, our kids can *claim* that they just never heard us. It's brutal, because we can't know for sure that they have heard us unless we happen to be standing directly in front of them, with eyes locked, screaming their name. It's maddening, and it only gets worse. This condition of selective hearing is something that all of us have to deal with, at least a good chunk of the time, as our kids are growing.

I've always found it hysterical that my kids could hear me talking to Dave about an ice cream craving from across the house while inside their bedroom with the door closed and earbuds in their ears. But yell to them from across the living room, eight feet away, to please get their backpack off the kitchen floor and all I'd get were crickets. Nothing. No response.

I know we all have these goals when we're starting out as parents to artfully craft, uh, I mean raise, these well-behaved, model little citizens who come when we call them, never talk back, and vacuum their rooms on a regular basis without being asked. It's every parent's dream, but it's a pipe dream. Sorry. The reality is that kids ignore their parents. It's the natural order of things. And that's what we need to remember.

I've had my own kids ignore me when I'm literally asking for a one-word answer. I've watched them respond to another parent or their teachers while they were totally ignoring me (because a child would never dare to ignore a teacher). Even though the communication breakdown happens gradually, it still happens. And it causes friction.

As far as I'm concerned, Charles Shulz was spot-on when he made all the adults in his *Peanuts* cartoons talk in garbled "waa-waa-waa" voices, because that's exactly what the average parent/child interaction looks like from the kid's perspective. From their angle, we use too many words to say what we need to say, everything we say sounds like we're mad, and we're usually interrupting some super-important free play.

Every one of us feels ignored somewhere along the way. While you may only be on the cusp of being tuned out by your kids, because they're still super dependent on you for just about everything, the time will inevitably come when your voice starts sounding like the shrill of a fax machine signal when you accidentally dial into someone's fax line. Like everything we go through with our kids as they age and mature, the communication gap will close back up. Eventually they come around and realize that it benefits them to listen to us. A lot. It takes a while for them to accept that. For a time, they just hear a lot of white noise.

📖 **From communication to curfews, parenting is just plain challenging. As we try to do our best, keep in mind that you must take care of yourself too.**

How We Sound Matters

We also have to consider how we sound to our kids when we're trying to get their attention. Are we nagging them? Do we sound angry or annoyed? Are we threatening them for not paying attention to us? How we get *and keep* their attention is completely up to us. Honestly, after almost twenty years as a parent, I can say, without any hesitation, that I spent too much time barking at my kids.

Ever take a step back and really listen to how you're talking to your kids? If we all did a little self-reflecting once in a while, I think we'd see pretty clearly that we don't always come across the way we think we do. In our heads we're gently coaxing our kids, but to them, we're full-on nagging, yelling, annoying, and pestering. And that's the crux of the communication problem. Luckily, there are things we can do to help ease the struggle on both sides.

We need to keep in mind that the kid brain gets easily engrossed—in everything. So even though we may want them to respond to us right away, they're not always able to because that piece of their brain hasn't developed yet. In case you haven't noticed, kids aren't always the best transitioners. We've all seen the fourth-grader who ignores the bell at the end of recess; he's just not done playing basketball. Or there's the tween daughter who needs to put down her phone and concentrate on homework, but she has a hard time making the switch.

There are some easy ways you can help keep your kids on task, like avoiding quick activity changes by giving a couple of early warnings before your kids need to stop an activity. You can also stop one activity during a natural break point and redirect them toward something else without making the change too drastic.

See, most kids respond to the news and not the weather. My kids certainly did when they were in grade school and really still do today. By that I mean be brief; be to the point, use simple, direct words, and be very, very specific. Most kids can't handle being saturated by directions, reprimands, and lectures. Just call them out on their behavior or give them the direction you need them to follow. Then step back and give them the chance to act. I repeat: step back and give them at least a second to transition. Do *not* throw a hissy if they don't instantly bolt up from the play table all attentive and ready to serve. Because it won't help.

Also, there's a great big difference between want and need. Which is why sometimes it's important for us to recognize if what we're asking of them is what we really *need* or just something we really *want*. You may need to step back and consider if what you're asking for can or should wait while Steven finishes building that super-cool Lego machine. In other words, don't interrupt your kid's creativity or space when you can give them that gift of time. So many of the things we ask our kids to do, like homework and chores and commitments, don't always have to get interrupted when we want something done. If our kids are genuinely involved in something like a research project but they forgot to fold their laundry, we can adjust our expectations a little because we see that they're engaged in doing something important. The simple solution is to offer our daughter the chance to finish what she's working on and then fit the chore in after. Win-win.

It's important for us to recognize if what we're asking of them is what we really *need*.

Another thing to keep in mind is that a lot of the push-back we get from our kids is driven by their need for attention. Which means that, some of the time, they're not responding to us because they're trying to get our attention. Because they're so young and immature, they often can't differentiate between negative attention and positive attention. To them, attention is attention. A good example is when six-year-old Lucy isn't ready to leave the park so she pretends to ignore us when we call her over to the car. She can hear us, and she knows exactly what we're asking, but she's pushing back as a way of making a stand.

Something else that's critical in terms of communicating with our kids is to stay calm—like Buddha calm. An anxious parent and a defiant kid do *not* mesh well. The minute my girls saw that I was riled up, they'd know I was vulnerable and they'd tune me out even more. The secret is to stay calm, even when you're not getting a response. Cool like the other side of the pillow cool. Because if we're in a Zen state of mind when we're trying to get our kids to cooperate, they'll be more inclined to listen.

Another trick you can try is making a game out of listening. This works great with kids who are about five to eight years old. If we make following directions and responding fun for our kids, then our kids are usually more apt to get with the program. Make listening fun by putting a positive incentive on the other end. Maybe they get to stay up five minutes later or watch ten minutes more of their cartoon, perhaps after they've cleaned up all their toys. Give them a carrot to reach for and they'll be more eager to behave—you know, some good old-fashioned motivation, which, by the way, is totally different than bribing our kids for listening and following directions. There's absolutely nothing wrong with incentivizing our kids for good behavior. In fact, it's incredibly effective. When we occasionally compensate them for doing what we need them to do, it helps them learn new skills. This is not a bribe. I repeat: this is not a bribe; it is a proven way to help our kids learn and keep our own sanity.

Bribes, well they're borne out of manipulation and, as a general rule, are very, very bad. When we lob out a bribe as a way of modifying our kids' behavior, we've just given our kids complete control over the situation. As soon as they associate their negative behavior with getting a kickback, we've lost the war. Bribes are almost always given out under duress, when our last nerve is fraying and about to snap. It's a horrible option that we never want to use. Honestly, it shouldn't even be in our arsenal to begin with, because once we cross over into bribing our kids to listen or behave or communicate with us, we've just taken the first tragic step towards raising an entitled kid.

Remember, developing good communication with our kids is a process—a long, tedious, and totally imperfect process. We have to be patient and stay the course. We have to work with our kids day in and day out to establish good communication patterns. Even though it's not easy, it can be done—and done well.

> **Developing good communication with our kids is a process—a long, tedious, and totally imperfect process.**

If patience, tolerance, and good role modeling don't work, there's another trick we can whip out: we can give them a little taste of their own Robitussin and ignore them right back. We can refuse to answer them when they call us and let them feel, firsthand, what it's like to be ignored. Start chopping veggies while they're trying to tell us something super-important just so they can know the feeling of being dismissed. While this might be a slightly more juvenile and tit-for-tat method of fostering good communication with our kids, it's a killer strategy that works almost every time. It's also a little dose of what can happen in the real world when you ignore people. The key here is to always have a chat afterward—a little debrief so they know why you ignored them. This is when the learning can happen. If their light bulb goes on, the tit-for-tat worked.

> 🛋 **Do onto others as they do onto you. Sometimes experiential learning is the best way to actually understand something. It is true that experience is the best teacher.**

Helping Tweens and Teens Listen (If That's Possible)

One thing we can pretty easily do is remember that our kids *think* they know everything. Right or wrong, it's just how a kid's mind works. They're sure they understand how to handle every situation and crisis, even when they're young, so they gradually start tuning us out as they start interacting with the rest of the world. This tuning out can sometimes translate to spending more time secluded in their room and acting stubborn or distant. But this kind of behavior is normal as our kids figure out who they are and how to interact with us now that they're older and a tiny bit wiser.

When both of my girls started consistently locking their bedroom doors in middle school, we decided it was time to establish some ground rules about when it was okay to have doors locked. They were no longer listening to us when we repeatedly asked them to keep their doors open unless they were getting changed. Instead, they started locking the door just to keep everyone out. And whenever we'd knock to come in, they'd take their sweet little time getting up off their bed, walking over to the door, and unlocking it. It got so bad it felt like we were standing outside their door waiting for ten minutes. So what did we do? We established some consequences that would get handed out if they kept locking their doors when they weren't getting dressed. And, just to give a sense of what it felt like to have to wait outside a locked door, we started locking *our door*. Constantly. Morning. Noon. And night. Whenever they'd try to barge in, our door was locked. It drove them crazy. Every single time it happened, we'd just calmly say, *getting dressed*. Then we'd take our sweet time walking over to the door. It didn't take too much of that to get our point across. Little by little, their doors were open and unlocked most of the day. (Plus, I think they knew that if they didn't get with the program, their doorknobs were going to be taken off to help prove the point.) Isn't it interesting that there are times we can communicate without saying a word?

When we're patient and disciplined in how we communicate with our kids, we *all* eventually learn how to talk to each other—and how to listen. (Which is equally as important.)

That's the thing—we have to remember that there's only so much processing our kids can do effectively—that any one of us can do effectively. The best piece of advice I can give anyone who's learning how to talk to their kids is to **just shut up and listen sometimes**. Not all the time, but sometimes for sure. Because the sooner we learn when to zip it and when to engage, the more effectively we'll be able to connect with our kids.

Oh yeah, and if absolutely none of that works (which is entirely possible), **just walk away**. Don't stand there hammering at your tween for the sake of resolving whatever conflict you're dealing with. (My own personal challenge.) Sometimes things need to stay unresolved for a little while until everyone can take a step back and reflect and, most importantly, cool down. This becomes more and more important as all the teenage hormones enter the scene.

> **Sometimes things need to stay unresolved for a little while until everyone can take a step back and reflect and, most importantly, cool down.**

Me, I've never been good with leaving things open-ended, certainly not with my kids. When we have arguments or disagreements, I'm inclined to hash things out until we reach a resolution. I keep saying the same thing over and over and over. In ten different ways and for way too long, hoping that we'll settle things. The problem with that is my kids would almost always tune me out after a very short time. This is the tendency of most kids. All of that talking becomes white noise that they can't or aren't interested in processing. And nothing gets accomplished.

Oftentimes sending everyone to their corners to regroup is the most effective solution. Although it sounds almost contradictory to walk away when we're trying to create a healthy dialogue with our kid, it's often the best approach. Why? Simply it saves us from saying something we'll regret or losing control or getting mad. In other words, it saves us from ourselves. We can't regret something we don't say or do.

> 💬 **There is never one perfect way of doing something when it comes to parenting.**

We need to stay cool when we're trying to communicate with our kids, remember who our audience is, and keep in mind that it's not always easy for our kids to communicate what's in their heads, especially when they're hormonal teens. Much of the time, they don't understand a lot of the new feelings and stress and emotions they're feeling yet. That's why the best approach for everyone is to slow things down and talk to each other when everyone's calm and at least semi-relaxed. Then try to put yourself in their shoes whenever you can and measure your words carefully, because the worst feeling is saying something you regret and that you can't take back.

Most importantly—and this goes way back to the beginning of the book where I talk about attitude—learning to harness your positivity will be your biggest asset as you navigate life as a parent. Being positive is the ultimate key to good communication.

Look, learning to communicate effectively within a family doesn't happen overnight. It takes work and time. And it definitely won't happen without everyone working together and following certain rules of engagement, like being a good listener, respecting each other's point of view, and being honest about their feelings. Because on the most basic level, we all need and want to be heard and understood. The earlier we establish open lines of communication with our kids, where they know that we care about what they have to say and we're going to take the time to listen, the more inclined they'll be to care about what we have to say too.

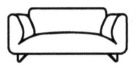

From the Couch of
Debra Fox Gansenberg MSW, LICSW

From communication to curfews, parenting is just plain challenging. As we try to do our best, keep in mind that you must take care of yourself too.

Whether we are working on communication or figuring out how to help with math, there are many things that we want to take into consideration when we approach parenting. Working with our children takes a lot of energy, patience, and time. Set yourself up for success and understand that life with children is like playing the game Whack-a-Mole, when one thing is settled another one pops up. To deal with the craziness, you must do some self-care.

Tip: Take care of yourself, Mom and Dad; rest, eat well, and get your sleep, because you are going to need a lot of energy both physically and emotionally. Come to the plate prepared and ready. Self-care is important because it impacts our performance as parents. Take time to decompress, relax, work out, and spend time with your friends. If we don't nurture ourselves, we can become resentful, easily frustrated, angry, and we are likely to quickly run out of patience, compassion, and understanding.

Tip: Stamina is important when it comes to parenting—it's a long haul. Pace yourself by stepping away and asking someone else to step in. Our daily jobs typically come with vacation time and sick days; however, our most important job, parenting, does not come with built-in benefits. Enlist a babysitter or relative to come take the kids so you can take a lunch break or dinner out. Many parents are apprehensive about bringing in help; do yourself a favor and ask that part of you to step back and make room for help. It will benefit you and your child in the long run.

Tip: As a parent, we are watching our child travel through various developmental stages. It is natural for their process to bring us back to our own process of growing up. Our past experiences definitely impact our behavior as parents, whether the experiences were good, bad, or indifferent. Take some time to reflect about your own upbringing; if there are memories or experiences that seem to get in the way of approaching parenting in a healthy way, take some time to look at that. Enlisting a therapist to process what comes up for you might help you take some of the things that can get in the way of being the best parent you want to be and put them in a better place.

Message: Be gentle to yourself, Mom and Dad, and take care of *you* because no one else will. Model good self-care and teach your children how important it is to be healthy mentally and physically so you can be your best self; that is great parenting all around.

Do onto others as they do onto you. Sometimes experiential learning is the best way to actually understand something. It is true that experience is the best teacher.

Tip: It is important to understand that when we actually feel something for our self it is internalized and the odds of remembering how you felt and what you learned are much greater. Learning by doing is a method that helps us take information and use it by putting it into action. If a child is asked to share but doesn't really know how that looks or feels, request that he *try it*. "Jayme, can you please share your softball glove with your friend Jake because he left his glove at his house?" Or "Michael, can you and Jonathan include Debra in your card game? Please show your sister what we discussed yesterday about including everyone." Take a lesson that you have taught verbally and create an opportunity to experience it.

Tip: Parents, if you have an idea or crafted a plan to implement in the home, put it into play. You will never know if your plan will work if you don't try it out. Kids don't have a chance to change if you only come up with a plan or idea. You need to teach the lesson or skill to them and then watch them learn and experience it to see if they understand. A behavioral plan for a child is a perfect example of thinking up an idea, creating a chart, teaching child behavior and expectations, and then letting them try it out. Watch your child, make adjustments if necessary, and then reward with kind words or actions to enforce the learned behavior. Over time they will master the behavior through continued experience.

There is never one perfect way of doing something when it comes to parenting.

As we finish up, it's most important to remember that parents are human. We are not perfect, which means we all make mistakes; learn from them and continue to grow. If we keep the same in mind when we think about our children, then this parenting thing should go pretty well. When you or your child make a mistake, remember, it's what you do with it that counts.

Tip: Kids have lots of needs and they vary from one child to the next. We are not superheroes, even if our kids think we are, so keep in mind that we cannot meet all of their needs and *that is okay*. The reality that we can't always get what we want or need is important for our kids to learn.

Tip: The most valuable thing to encourage when raising your children is communication in the home. As parents, we need to model how to express ourselves in order for our kids to see that it is important and safe to do so. Kids will learn that they have a voice and what they have to say is valuable so that others can understand what they are thinking along their journey in life. Finding your voice is empowering; the younger they learn to communicate, the more successful they will be in all aspects of their life as adults.

Tip: Create opportunities for teaching and practicing with your children all the various skills that have been spoken about in this book. Don't assume they know how or why to do something. Teach expectations, model the behavior, and be patient while they learn. Practice makes almost perfect.

Message: Each child is different, their needs are different, and the way they need to be parented will vary. Walking away, talking it out, giving them space, rewarding them, punishing them—the recipe is never exactly the same. We are people with our own history, skill set, and expectations. As you come together in the family of origin that you have created, remember that everyone is human. Take it slow and be gentle to yourself as you raise your perfectly imperfect child.

Afterword

When Dave and I started our family over twenty years ago, we were more or less clueless about how to be parents. We had only been married for four years, so we were basically kids ourselves, and even though we had our own parents and family nearby to help guide us, the ultimate responsibility of figuring everything out and navigating parenthood was on us. We knew we were both pretty capable people, but it was still a super-intimidating thought.

Sure, we read plenty of parenting books and all of them gave us at least a vague sense of what parenthood would be like. But there was nothing out there that talked honestly, in an unfiltered way, about all the *other* stuff that goes along with being a parent. You know, the stuff like kid drama and participation trophies and how it feels when our kids start giving us attitude, or what it's like that first time we get a door slammed in our face. That was the kind of insight we really needed, but it didn't exist.

Flash forward a bunch of years after our girls were born and I'd like to say that we eventually found a rhythm. And in a lot of ways we did. We got used to having a little person in tow all the time and always sleeping with one ear open. We got comfortable putting our daughters' best interests ahead of our own. We figured out that double (and sometimes triple) diapering our girls meant that we'd always have a spare Huggies when we were out for the day. We learned that it's way easier to make five salami sandwiches on Sunday afternoon and freeze them for the week than it is to get up early to make a sandwich every morning before school. And we learned that when you speak your mind to your kid during a conflict and then walk away, they'll usually come to you first to apologize.

But we also learned that so much of parenting is subjective and freeform and unpredictable—that no matter how badly we wanted our kids to be happy all the time, life just doesn't work that way. We learned that just because a discipline strategy works for one family doesn't mean it'll work across the board. We figured out that we've *got* to let our kids fail and fall and be sad, because wrapped within those experiences are some of life's greatest lessons. Because when we fall and get up again or when we're sad and find happiness again, we appreciate it so much more.

Ultimately, we came to realize our kids are going to find their tribe and their way by tons of trial and error. But they *will* find it. We learned that all the best-laid plans and hopes and dreams we have for our kids are usually very different from how things really end up. That's why we have to be nimble and adaptable and open-minded as often as we can.

The most important thing we learned (and we're still learning) is that no kid, no parent, and no family is perfect, no matter how hard we all try. We're not always going to get it right, and our kids aren't always going to be the model little citizens we want them to be—because we're all a work in progress. That was a super-powerful nugget of parenting truth—so powerful that I started writing about it in my nationally syndicated opinion/humor column *It Is What It Is*. Then people everywhere started responding to the idea, saying it gave them the reality check they needed to loosen up and dial down their anxiety levels. Readers told me that once they stopped expecting their kids to be perfect and just let them be kids, there was a noticeable shift in the family dynamic for the better. So I kept writing and people kept responding.

Then Familius and I found each other and realized we had a shared mission of making families happy. So I pitched them an idea for a book about how to raise perfectly imperfect kids and be okay with it, and they liked what they heard. That's how *How to Raise Perfectly Imperfect Kids . . . And Be OK with It* came to be.

So thanks for being here. Thanks for being open to the idea that perfection is a myth and that even though we all want to get it right 100 percent of the time, we just won't. But that's okay. Because while none of us has the patented blueprint for how to build the perfect kid, every one of us has the power to embrace and nurture the kid we have and celebrate their screw-ups as much as we celebrate their wins. In the end, our attitude is what matters most. And it's really all just about the climb.

Acknowledgments

From Lisa Sugarman:

Now, I'd be a horrible person if I didn't acknowledge all the beautiful humans who helped me bring this project to life. So first and foremost, I need to thank my husband, Dave, for relentlessly motivating me to pursue every dream I've ever had since forever. For supporting my insatiable need to write my column, this book (and others), and for picking up the slack when my head was buried deep in my laptop for hours and weeks and days and years. You're my boy, Blue, and this book would never have happened without your unending love, support, and encouragement. No one loves you like I do.

To my best friends and daughters, Riley and Libby, for tolerating and embracing my *special* kind of crazy since the second you were born, even though you didn't really have a choice. (And for swearing that, someday, you'd read all of my books.) I love you for letting me practice this parenting thing on you, for better or for worse. And for being the subjects of more columns than I can even count, in spite of never wanting to be. And for giving me enough beautiful material to write about until the end of time. You're the kids of my dreams, and I'm blessed to call you mine. And I have to say, I couldn't be prouder of how you two turned out. This book is for you. Please share. Mommy loves you.

To my mom, Sandy, the true Queen of All that Matters, who's read and edited every single word I've written since I was five years old. You've celebrated everything that's ever been important to me all my life, and I love you for it more than words. You always told me I could, so I did. And thankfully for me, you've been right by my side through every big and small moment, milestone, and decision in my life, guiding me by offering the best example of what it means to be a truly good person and live your best life. Thank you for giving me the strength to believe that what I had to say matters. And for always being there knowing exactly what to say whenever I doubted myself. This project isn't mine, it's ours. And you are, and have always been, the wind beneath my wings.

To my in-laws, Stan and Evelyne, and my sister- and brother-in-law, Dianne and Steve, and my step-dad, Ronnie, and my extended family near and far who sent constant love and faith and made me feel like I could do anything. Your love and support and pride in me has meant everything. You've never been in laws or steps—you've always been the real McCoys. I hit the jackpot the day you each came into my life.

To my friends—my tribe—who gave me the confidence to believe that I had something worth saying. There are just no words. You're my people and I adore you.

To my friends at Shubie's, my office-away-from-the-office, thank you for saving me a stool year after year as I mooched power from behind the counter, drank bottomless mugs of coffee, and spent endless hours doing what I love. I've written three books under your roof, and I hope to write a hundred more. I'm grateful for all the encouragement, love, and support. It's meant the world to me, and so do you. And I swear that I'll start contributing to the electric bill as soon as this book hits the *New York Times* Bestseller List.

To my editors, Michele Robbins and Brooke Jorden, who hung in for the long haul and helped make this book better than I ever could have on my own. Thank you for helping me flesh out the best possible version of my book. To Derek George, who dressed it up for the world and made it look beautiful. And to Kate Farrell, my marketing and PR genius and *treasured* friend, who got my book into everyone's hands, even when they didn't know they needed it. And to all the other dedicated minds and hands behind the scenes at Familius, without whom my books wouldn't exist. I can never thank you all enough.

And to my girl, Debra Fox Gansenberg, my beautiful and brilliant friend since the fourth grade. Thank you for stepping up at the eleventh hour and jumping onboard this bullet train when I had an epiphany that you belonged in this book. *How to Raise Perfectly Imperfect Kids . . .*

And Be OK with It is more than I ever imagined it could be because you're a part of it. And we're just getting started.

Finally, to my publishers, Christopher and Michele Robbins at Familius, for seeing the vision and potential of *How to Raise Perfectly Imperfect Kids . . . And Be OK with It* and for giving me a chance. Thank you for believing in me and in our shared vision of making families happy. Your faith in me has changed my life. Because without you, all these words would still just be ideas cluttering up my head. Here's to writing millions more words together.

From Debra Fox Gansenberg:

This chapter of my life and career would not be possible without the help and support of so many people. Whether it has been words of encouragement, your help and support, or a pardon for being too busy, all has been appreciated and not gone unrecognized. Through my journey you all have taught me that life isn't always perfect, that raising a family isn't always pretty, and that I am very fortunate to spend my life doing what I love each and every day; thank you.

Wally, you might not have written any words to this book but you, along with the rest of my family and friends, have contributed in many ways to make this fabulous book happen. Thank you for modeling for our children what an amazing support system should look like and how to encourage your loved ones to follow their dreams. You are selfless, willing, and ready to do what you had to for our family so that I am able do what I love to do as a professional working wife and mother. I could not fully be who I am today without your endless love and support, and for that I am forever grateful. I love you.

Jacob, Benjamin, and Adam, I am the luckiest member of the Ganz Gang because I have three amazing cheerleaders everywhere I go in life. You have taught me more than you will ever know. Your lessons continue to guide me on my journey in helping others. To see the excitement, encouragement, and pride you have for what I do in my life keeps me going each and every day. I hope you will someday be able to look back on your journey, as I do, and know you have lived a happy and fulfilling life. The three of you make me so proud and make it look like I actually know what I am doing. I love you all more than you will ever know.

To my parents, thank you for giving me the gift of your love and support necessary to find my way in life. You provided me with the resources and education necessary to become the professional woman I am today, and for that I am grateful. Thank you for believing in me and teaching me to believe in myself; both have provided me the ability to succeed in all the areas of my life. Mom, we took a journey together to make a dream come true. We created NBCS as a place to do what we love while being a resource to others. Thank you for helping me build a foundation for my future and live my many dreams. I could not have taken this journey without you. Thank you for all that you are in my life; I love you both.

To my siblings, in-law family, colleagues, and community, together you all fill my life with purpose and meaning. There isn't enough ink or paper to list the many people that have been part of my journey, so if you don't see your name know you are so loved and on my list of people that I am forever grateful for both personally and profession-ally. Thank you all for your kindness, words of encouragement, and endless support. I could never imagine finding my way without all of you touching my life in some way. Thank you for making my world so wonderful.

Michele and Christopher Robbins and the Familius family, thank you for your support and encouragement as you welcomed me into uncharted territory. Adding "author" to my credentials is a privilege, and I have the Familius family to thank for giving me this opportu-nity to share my life's lessons and professional knowledge with those looking for guidance and resources to live a family life that is happy, healthy, and successful for everyone.

Lisa Sugarman, who would have ever thought that our lives would lead us to this incredible place. You are one impressive and knowl-edgeable human being with endless energy and enthusiasm. You have built a life that is filled with a magnificent family, inspiring accom-plishments, and a community of incredible people. I feel privileged to be part of your circle in life and appreciate your belief in me and my abilities. I look forward to our future endeavors, because, with you as part of my life, anything is possible . . . I am an author, and I have you to thank!

Notes

1. "2016 Children's Mental Health Report," *Child Mind Institute*, accessed March 25, 2019, http://childmind.org/report/2016-childrens-mental-health-report/.
2. Paula Durlofsky, "The Benefits of Emotional Intelligence," *Psychcentral*, July 8, 2018, https://psychcentral.com/blog/the-benefits-of-emotional-intelligence/.
3. Erin Gabriel, "Understanding Emotional Intelligence and Its Effects on Your Life," *CNN.com*, updated July 26, 2018, https://www.cnn.com/2018/04/11/health/improve-emotional-intelligence/index.html.
4. John M. Grohol, "IQ Test," *Psychcentral*, accessed February 24, 2019, https://psychcentral.com/encyclopedia/what-is-an-iq-test/.
5. "Emotional Intelligence," *Pychology Today*, accessed February, 24, 2019, https://www.psychologytoday.com/us/basics/emotional-intelligence.
6. Keld Jensen, "Intelligence Is Overrated: What You Really Need to Succeed," *Forbes*, April 12, 2012, https://www.forbes.com/sites/keldjensen/2012/04/12/intelligence-is-overrated-what-you-really-need-to-succeed/#65119c6eb6d2.
7. "The Joys of Doing Nothing," *Scholastic*, accessed February, 24, 2019, https://www.scholastic.com/parents/kids-activities-and-printables/activities-for-kids/arts-and-craft-ideas/joys-doing-nothing.html.

8. "AAP Clinical Report: Young Children Risk Injury in Single-Sport Specialization," *American Academy of Pediatrics*, August 29, 2016, https://www.aap.org/en-us/about-the-aap/aap-press-room/Pages/AAP-Clinical-Report-Young-Children-Risk-Injury-in-Single-Sport-Specialization.aspx.

9. "Punishment vs. Logical Consequences," *Responsive Classroom*, September 2, 2011, https://www.responsiveclassroom.org/punishment-vs-logical-consequences/.

10. Annie Stuart, "Divide and Conquer Household Chores," *Web MD*, accessed February 20, 2019, https://www.webmd.com/parenting/features/chores-for-children#1.

11. Fulghum, Robert. *All I Really Need to Know I Learned in Kindergarten*. New York: Ballantine Books, 2004, 4-6.

12. Fulghum, 4–6.

13. Resnick, Mitchel. "Kindergarten Is the Model for Lifelong Learning," *Edutopia*, May 27, 2009, https://www.edutopia.org/kindergarten-creativity-collaboration-lifelong-learning.

14. Bob Livingstone, "Why It Is Important for Our Children to Have Friends," *Mentalhelp.net*, accessed February 28, 2019, https://www.mentalhelp.net/blogs/why-it-is-important-for-our-children-to-have-friends/.

15. Eileen Kennedy-Moore and Mark S. Lowenthal, *Smart Parenting for Smart Kids: Nurturing Your Child's True Potential*, 2011, San Francisco: Jossey-Bass, 2011, 44.

16. Rebecca Bowen, "Social Skills: 5 Tips to Help Shy Kids Make Friends," *The Inspired Treehouse*, September 30, 2015, https://theinspiredtreehouse.com/social-skills-5-tips-to-help-shy-kids-make-friends/.

17. "10 Simple Ways to Improve Children's Behavior (Home and School)," *Education and Behavior*, December 22, 2016, http://www.educationandbehavior.com/how-to-discipline-a-child-with-behavior-problems/.

18. Allan L. Beane, *The Bully Free Classroom: Over 100 Tips and Strategies for Teachers K–8*, Golden Valley: Free Spirit Pub, 2005, 55.

19. Robin Nixon and Robert Roy Britt, "10 Facts Every Parent Should Know about Their Teen's Brain," *Livescience*, March 31, 2016, https://www.livescience.com/13850-10-facts-parent-teen-brain.html.

20. "Understanding the Teen Brain," *Stanford Children's Health*, accessed February 28, 2019, http://www.stanfordchildrens.org/en/topic/default?id=understanding-the-teen-brain-1-3051.

21. Eric Fluckey, "Why Sarcasm Is so Great," *Life*, December 6, 2017, https://www.huffpost.com/entry/why-sarcasm-is-so-great_n_7887342?ec_carp=7562404672358311562.

22. Richard Chin. "The Science of Sarcasm? Yeah, Right." *Smithsonian.com*, November 14, 2011, http://www.smithsonianmag.com/science-nature/the-science-of-sarcasm-yeah-right-25038/?no-ist.

23. Chin, "The Science of Sarcasm."

24. Mary L. Gavin, "Encouraging Your Child's Sense of Humor," *KidsHealth.org*, June 1, 2015, http://kidshealth.org/en/parents/child-humor.html.

25. "Examples of Sarcasm," *Your Dictionary*, accessed February 28, 2019, https://examples.yourdictionary.com/examples-of-sarcasm.html.

26. Jacqueline Howard, "When Kids Get Their First Cell Phones around the World," *CNN.com*, December 11, 2017, https://www.cnn.com/2017/12/11/health/cell-phones-for-kids-parenting-without-borders-explainer-intl/index.html.

27. Natasha Singer, "Education Disrupted: How Google Took Over the Classroom," *New York Times*, May 13, 2017, https://www.nytimes.com/2017/05/13/technology/google-education-chromebooks-schools.html.

28. Amy Morin, "The Harmful Effects of Too Much Screen Time for Kids," *Verywell Family*, updated November 3, 2018, https://www.verywellfamily.com/the-negative-effects-of-too-much-screen-time-1094877.

About the Authors

Lisa Sugarman is the author of the nationally syndicated opinion column *It Is What It Is*, featured in over five hundred GateHouse Media, Inc. newspapers and websites around the country.

Along with being a long-time columnist and humorist for GateHouse, she is also a regular contributor to *Grown and Flown*, *Hot Moms Club*, *MommingHubb*, *This Mama Wines*, and *Care.com*. The mom of two daughters, wife to her summer-after-high-school-graduation sweetheart (David), and author, Lisa understands that we're all perfectly imperfect works in progress. Especially our kids.

She is also the author of the *Boston Globe* Local Bestseller *Untying Parent Anxiety: 18 Myths That Have You in Knots—And How to Get Free* and *LIFE: It Is What It Is*, a collection of fifty favorite *It Is What It Is* opinion columns; available on Amazon, Barnes & Noble.com, and at specialty bookstores in the Boston area.

Apart from her life as a mom and a writer, Lisa is also an *avid* runner, skier, snowboarder, and paddleboarder who loves fitness and movement in all its forms. You can find her at stupid-o'clock in the morning running the hills on Summit Avenue in Brookline, Massachusetts, or the stairs at Harvard Stadium every Monday, Wednesday, and Friday morning with her tribe of fitness yahoos, November Project.

Debra Fox Gansenberg, MSW, LICSW, is the founder and owner of New Beginnings Counseling Service, P.C., located around the North Shore of Boston. She has a twenty-five-year history working in the mental health field as a skilled clinical psychotherapist and business owner specializing in individual, couple, group, and family therapy.

Debra has also been the Director of School Services for NBCS for twenty plus years and she has customized and implemented school-based counseling services for Pre-K through twelfth grade. Debra enjoys public speaking, as well as designing and implementing programming for various topics and audiences. She lives north of Boston with her husband and three sons.

About Familius

Visit Our Website: www.familius.com

Familius is a global-trade publishing company that publishes books and other content to help families be happy. We believe that the family is the fundamental unit of society and that happy families are the foundation of a happy life. We recognize that every family looks different, and we passionately believe in helping all families find greater joy. To that end, we publish books for children and adults that invite families to live the Familius Nine Habits of Happy Family Life: *love together, play together, learn together, work together, talk together, heal together, read together, eat together,* and *laugh together.* Founded in 2012, Familius is located in Sanger, California.

Join Our Family

There are lots of ways to connect with us! Subscribe to our newsletters at www.familius.com to receive uplifting daily inspiration, essays from our Pater Familius, a free ebook every month, and the first word on special discounts and Familius news.

Get Bulk Discounts

If you feel a few friends and family might benefit from what you've read, let us know and we'll be happy to provide you with quantity discounts. Simply email us at orders@familius.com.

Connect

Facebook: www.facebook.com/paterfamilius
Twitter: @familiustalk, @paterfamilius1
Pinterest: www.pinterest.com/familius
Instagram: @familiustalk

The most important work you ever do will be within the walls of your own home.

CPSIA information can be obtained
at www.ICGtesting.com
Printed in the USA
FSHW011828310719